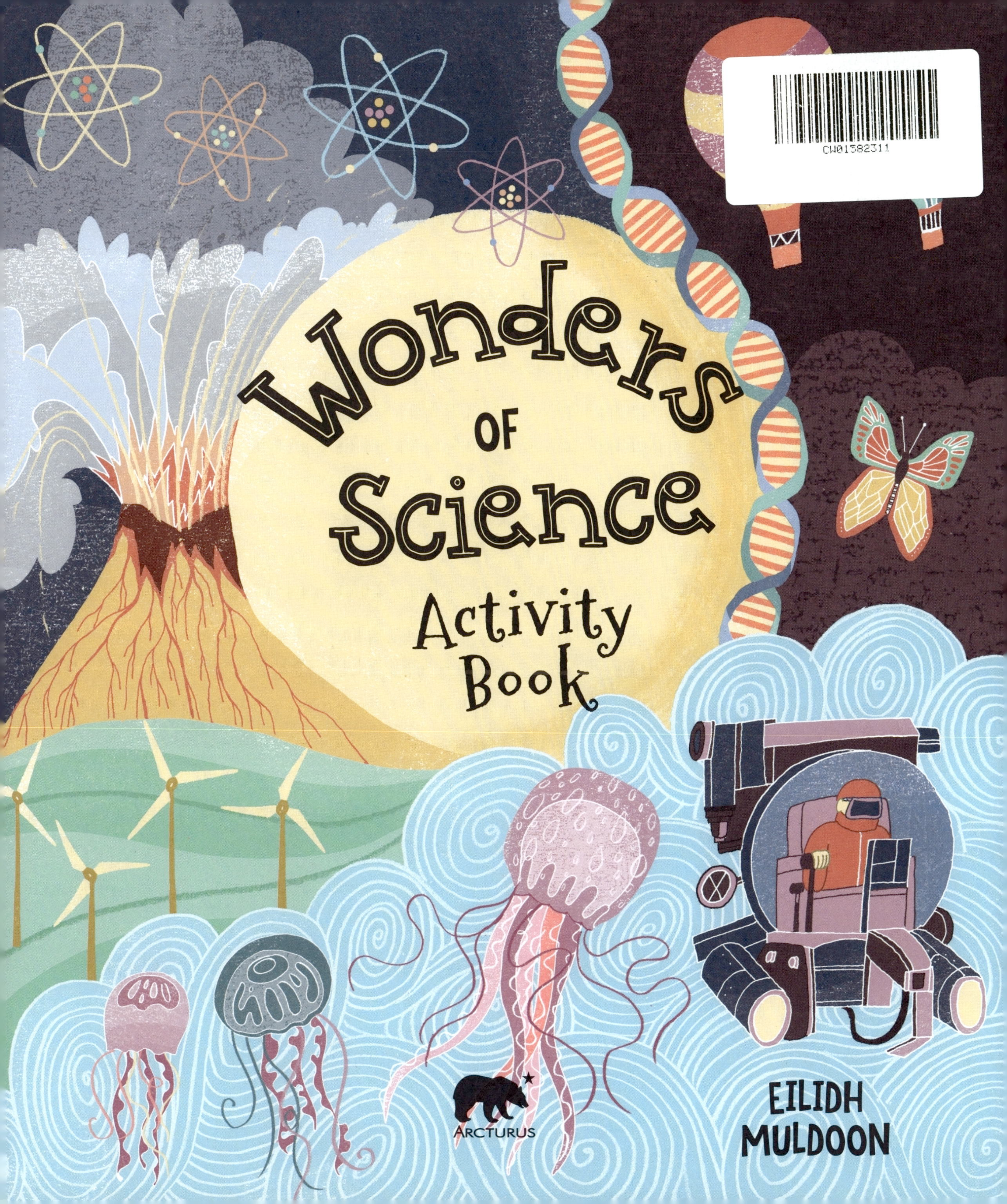
Wonders of Science
Activity Book
ARCTURUS
EILIDH MULDOON

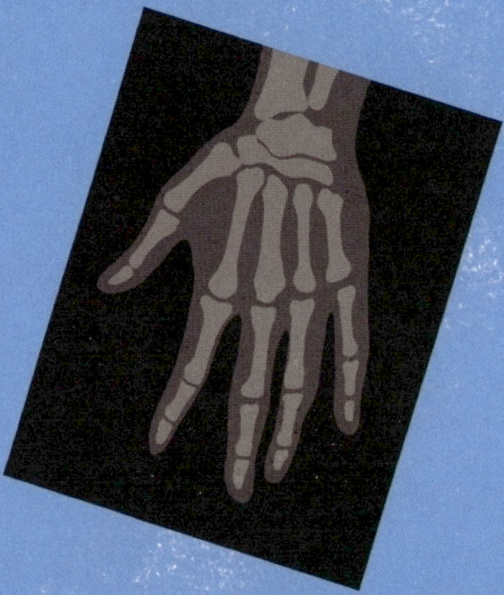

ARCTURUS

This edition published in 2023 by Arcturus Publishing Limited
26/27 Bickels Yard, 151–153 Bermondsey Street,
London SE1 3HA



Author: Lisa Regan
Illustrator: Eilidh Muldoon
Designer: Supriya Sahai
Editors: Becca Clunes, Lydia Halliday
Design manager: Jessica Holliland
Editorial manager: Joe Harris

ISBN: 978-1-3988-1667-1
CH010449NT
Supplier 29, Date 0223, PI 00003446

Printed in China

STEM
SCIENCE TECHNOLOGY ENGINEERING MATHEMATICS

**What is STEM?**

STEM is a world-wide initiative that aims to cultivate an interest in Science, Technology, Engineering, and Mathematics, in an effort to promote these disciplines to as wide a variety of students as possible.

# Wonders of Science

Prepare to be amazed by the wonders of science! This book explores the physics, chemistry, and biology that make our wonderful world work. You'll find out which metals are magnetic, how a food chain works, where the wheel was first used, and why a boat floats on water. The fun puzzles on each page will reinforce your understanding of science and the amazing facts will make you look again at the world around you.

# CONTENTS

# MATTER

Everything in the universe is made of matter. You are made of matter, and so are your clothes, your food and drink, the oceans, the Sun and Moon...everything. Matter is made of atoms, which are tiny particles that join together to make solids, liquids, and gases (see page 10).

Atoms are themselves made of smaller particles called protons, neutrons, and electrons. Different elements have different numbers of these particles. Find the matching pairs among these atoms.

EONYGX

ONIR

OGDL

ERVILS

NONE

Rearrange the letters to find the name of each of these elements.

## Purely Elemental

An element is a pure substance that contains a single type of atom. These include gases such as hydrogen and argon, solids such as copper and lead, and few liquids such as bromine and mercury.

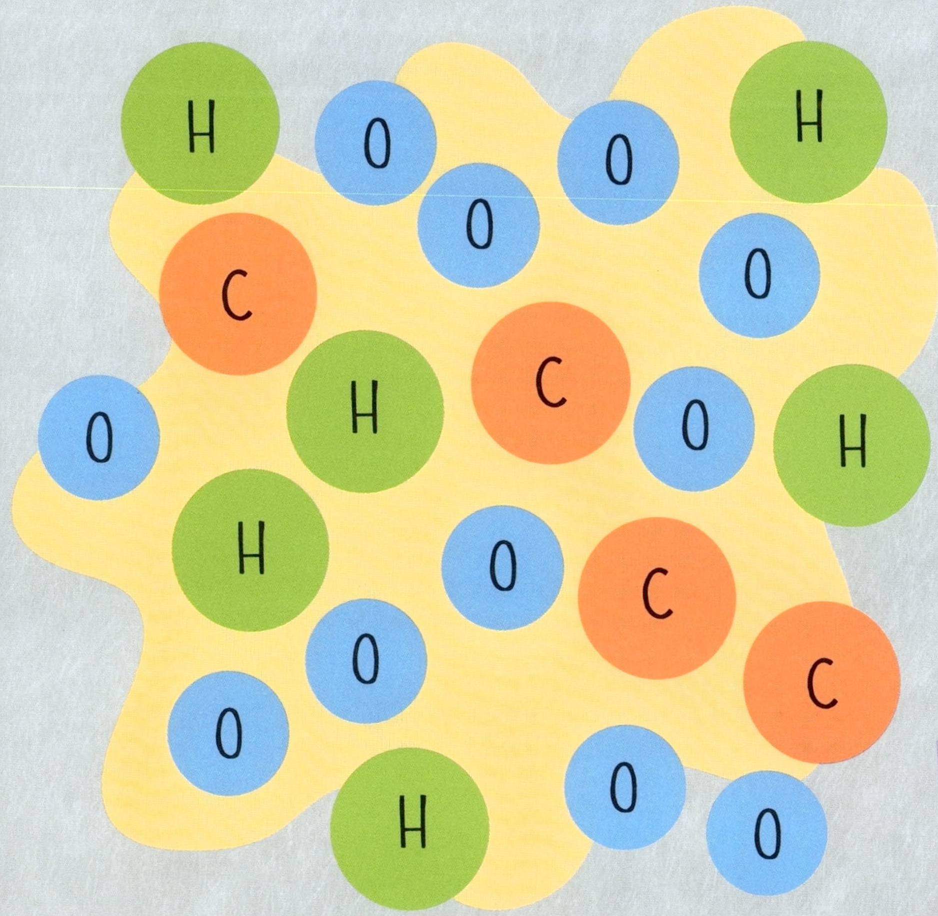


## Molecules

A molecule is two or more atoms that have bonded together. The atoms can be from different elements. For instance, two hydrogen atoms and one oxygen atom make a molecule of water. Scientists use letters to represent elements, so the chemical formula for water is $H_2O$. Carbon dioxide is another common molecule and it has the formula $CO_2$: two oxygen atoms bonded to a carbon atom.

If these atoms bonded together, how many molecules of water and carbon monoxide would there be?

If every person on the planet was the size of one atom, then all 7.8 billion of us would take up less space than a grain of sugar.

# MATERIALS

We are surrounded by things made of different materials such as plastic, metal, cloth, wood, glass, or rock. Some materials are natural, while others are manufactured.

# Fit for Purpose

Materials are chosen for their properties, such as whether they are strong, soft, smooth, see-through, or flexible.

Some of these properties have technical descriptions. Match each property to its definition.

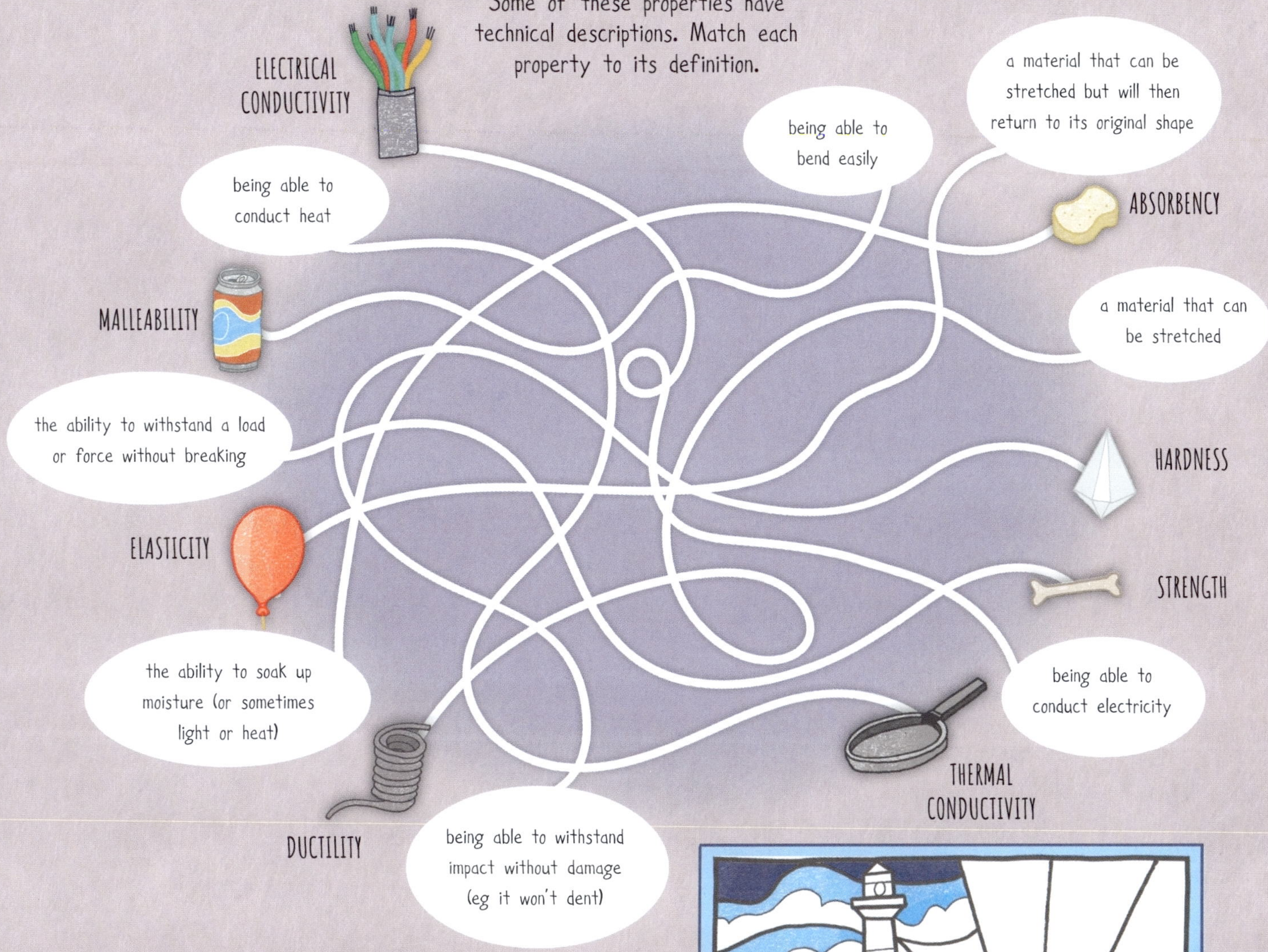


# Amazing Material

Glass has several useful properties—you can often see through it, it doesn't easily melt, and (when thick enough) it is hard and doesn't break easily. Glass is made mostly of sand, heated to a very high temperature. To make stained glass, metals are added at its liquid stage, giving it different shades. Finish this beautiful stained-glass window.

# STATES OF MATTER

Matter (see page 6) can exist in different forms, known as states. The most common are solid, liquid, and gas.

See how many times you can find each word hidden in the containers. The words can appear down or left to right, but not diagonally or backward.

| | | | | | | | | | | | | | |
|---|---|---|---|---|---|---|---|---|---|---|---|---|---|
| L | I | D | S | O | L | D | D | I | S | S | S | O | L |
| S | O | S | L | I | D | S | S | D | O | O | L | I | D |
| I | D | O | O | S | S | O | I | D | L | L | S | O | L |
| O | S | L | S | O | L | I | S | O | L | I | D | S | S |
| I | O | I | O | S | O | L | L | I | I | D | S | O | O |
| I | L | D | L | I | S | O | L | I | D | S | D | L | L |

| | | | | | | | | | |
|---|---|---|---|---|---|---|---|---|---|
| S | A | G | A | A | G | A | G | S | G |
| G | G | S | S | G | A | G | S | A | G |
| A | S | A | G | A | G | A | G | S | A |
| S | A | A | A | G | G | A | S | A | S |
| A | S | G | G | A | A | G | S | S | A |
| G | G | A | G | A | A | A | S | G | G |
| G | S | G | A | S | G | G | G | A | S |
| A | S | S | S | G | G | A | A | G | G |
| G | A | G | A | A | S | A | G | A | A |

L I Q
I Q L
D I I
L I D Q I
I Q L U Q
L Q U I I L I
I U I L D I D
I L I Q U I D U I
I U D L Q D U L I
Q D L I Q U I D Q

The particles in solids, liquids, and gases have different amounts of energy. They behave in different ways; for example, solids have a fixed shape and can't flow.

## Taking Shape

Liquids take the shape of the container they are stored in.

Find one container here that is different from all the others.

## All Change

States of matter can be changed, usually by heating or cooling a substance. Many solids melt, or change to liquids, when they are heated.

Can you draw pictures of water in its three states?

# CHEMICAL REACTIONS

Things around us are made up of atoms (see page 6) that join to make elements and compounds. They exist as many different substances, which we call chemicals. Chemicals can be combined to make new substances, or can be broken down into other substances.

Find the new substance that the chemist created this morning.

IT IS NOT AT THE END OF A ROW.
IT DOES NOT HAVE A STOPPER.
IT IS NEXT TO A PURPLE CONTAINER.

During chemical reactions, bonds between atoms are formed or broken. The substances that take part in the reaction are called reactants. The substances produced are known as the products. No atoms are created or destroyed during a reaction, but they are rearranged.

## No Going Back

Chemical reactions take place between the ingredients when you're baking a cake. There is no way you could reverse the actions to get back to flour, sugar, eggs, and butter.

Follow the arrows to get from bowl to beautiful chocolate cake. You will need to land on each ingredient once, in any order: flour, baking soda, sugar, butter, egg, and chocolate.

Lots of chemical reactions involve heat, to begin or speed up the reaction.

## Changing, not Reacting

Some changes are physical, not chemical. No new chemicals are made. Physical changes include freezing, melting, dissolving, and boiling.

Spot six differences between these two pictures.

# ROCKS AND MINERALS

From mighty mountains to tiny pebbles on a beach, the Earth is littered with rocks and rocky formations. All rocks are made of minerals—naturally occurring solids with a crystal structure inside.

Mount Rushmore is made of a type of hard rock called granite. It is home to the famous carving of four Presidents of the United States of America.

Can you find five differences between these pictures of the sculpture?

# City of Stone

The ancient city of Petra in Jordan is carved into the soft sandstone cliffs. It was built more than 2,200 years ago and much of it still survives today. Draw a mirror image here to complete the picture of this building.

# Precious Gems

Some minerals occur naturally as gemstones and are prized for their beauty. Fit these gems back into the grid so that each row, column, and minigrid contains one of each type.

# FOSSILS

A fossil is the preserved remains of an ancient living thing. Fossils are found in rocks, formed in the shape of objects that were buried and squashed under layers of sediment. Everything we know about extinct creatures, such as dinosaurs, is from fossils.

Match each of these dinosaurs to its young.

The fossils of teeth, bones, shells, and so on are called body fossils. The fossils of footprints and other evidence of activity are called trace fossils.

# In the Field

People who study fossils are called paleontologists. They learn about things that existed millions of years ago, and study how they lived and became extinct.

A

C

Find the tool kit that contains every item this paleontologist needs.

B

## Ocean Giant

Megalodon was an enormous prehistoric shark that became extinct around 3.6 million years ago. Based on the size of its fossil teeth, scientists think it grew up to 20 m (65 ft) long and had fins the size of an adult human!

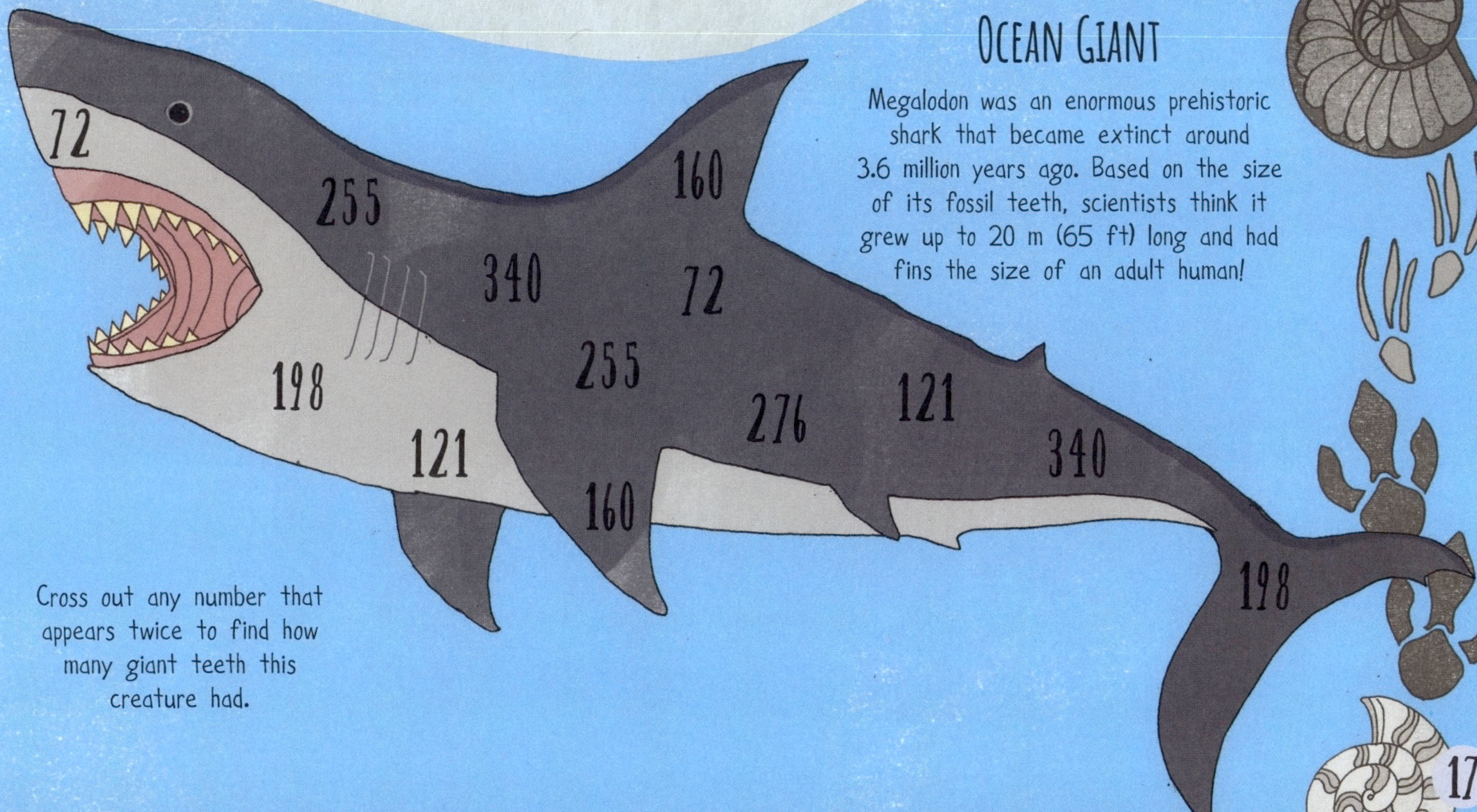


Cross out any number that appears twice to find how many giant teeth this creature had.

# HEAT

Heat is a kind of energy that is caused by the movement of atoms. Hot things contain more energy than cold ones. Some animals warm their bodies using heat from the Sun, but mammals and birds make heat from food.

Heat is a form of infrared radiation. A thermal imaging camera converts the infrared radiation into visible images.

You can see the hot and cold areas in these thermal images; but can you spot six differences between the two pictures?

# Cold... Colder... Coldest

Taking away heat energy from a substance makes it cool down. If you could take away all the energy, the atoms would stop moving altogether. This is the lowest temperature possible and it has a special name.

| A | B | C | D | E | F | G | H | I | J | K | L | M |
|---|---|---|---|---|---|---|---|---|---|---|---|---|
| Z | | | | | | | | | | | | |
| N | O | P | Q | R | S | T | U | V | W | X | Y | Z |
| | | | | | | | | | | C | B | A |

Complete the code and then use it to find out the name of the lowest possible temperature.

ZYHLOFGV AVIL

# Feeling Hot

In science, heat is defined as the flow of energy from one area to another. A hot item gives away its energy to a cooler item.

Divide these squares into groups of four. All the groups must be the same shape and they must all contain a campfire.

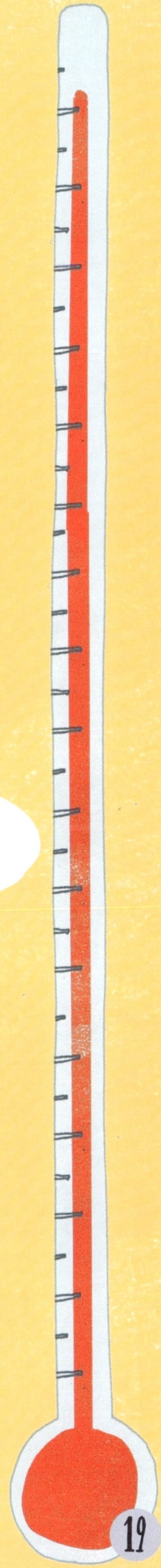

# LIGHT

Light is a type of energy we can see. Nearly all our light comes from the Sun. It travels in straight lines called waves; that's why we can't see round corners. However, light changes path when it hits objects. Shiny surfaces reflect light and make it bounce back toward the viewer.

Find six mistakes in the reflected part of this picture.

Starting with 100, subtract all of the numbers around the picture to find out how many minutes it takes for the Sun's light to reach us on Earth.

# White Light

White, or visible light, is actually made up of red, orange, yellow, green, blue, indigo, and violet rays. That's what we see when a beam of light splits to form a rainbow. Use the dots to help you fill in the picture correctly.

# A Bright Idea

Before the invention of the lightbulb, people lit candles to see after dark. It wasn't until the second half of the 1800s that inventors managed to produce electric lightbulbs, which changed the way people live.

How many lightbulbs are in this pile?

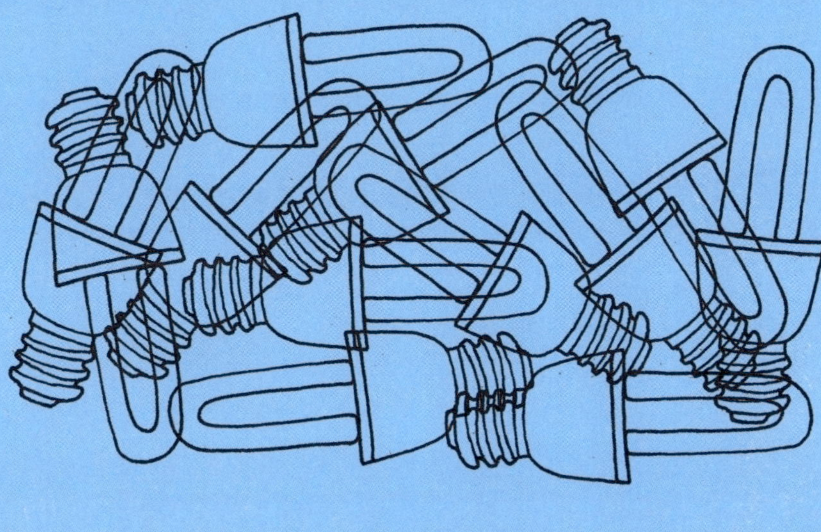

# SOUND

Sounds are made when objects vibrate, sending invisible waves through the air. Our ears change these waves into messages that can be understood by our brain. Musical instruments create harmonious (pleasant) sounds in a variety of ways.

Cross out the instruments with strings and the instruments you blow. Then, read the letters on the ones that are left to discover the name for instruments that you hit.

The oldest surviving musical instruments are all types of flute.

## MEGA EARS

Human ears are not as sensitive as those of some animals. We can't hear sounds with very low pitch (infrasound) or very high pitch (ultrasound). Low sounds travel farther than high sounds. Elephants—who hear very low sounds—can communicate with each other at distances over 10 km (6 miles).

Put these elephants in order, from largest to smallest.

Sounds can be caused by a glass falling on the floor, a car zooming past, a volcano erupting ... anything that causes vibrations. Sound can travel through solids, liquids, and gases, but at different speeds.

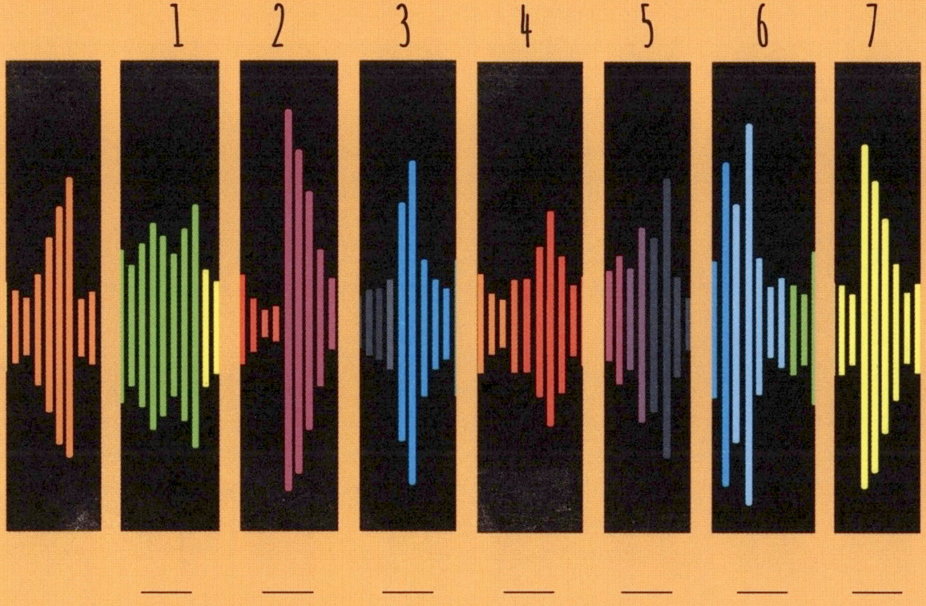


## MAKING WAVES

An oscilloscope is a way of displaying sound. The longer the bars are, the louder the sound.

Put these sections back in order following the different shades. The first orange one has been done for you.

# ENERGY

Think about your daily routine. What types of energy are involved? Exercise uses movement—or "kinetic"—energy. Baking uses heat, and gaming uses electrical energy.

Energy is never lost or destroyed, it just changes from one form to another. So, chemical energy in food is changed to kinetic energy when we move.

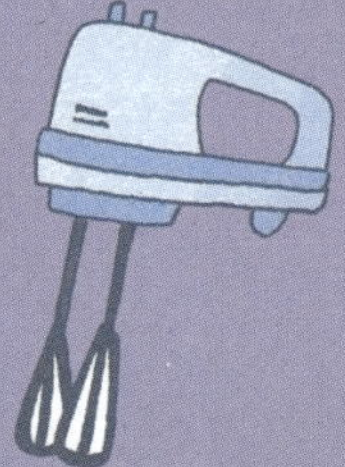

Use the clues and check the boxes to work out which person is doing which activity, and where they are.

NANCY IS NOT GAMING.
THE PERSON BAKING IS AT HOME.
THE GAMER IS NOT HENRY.
NANCY IS AT SCHOOL.

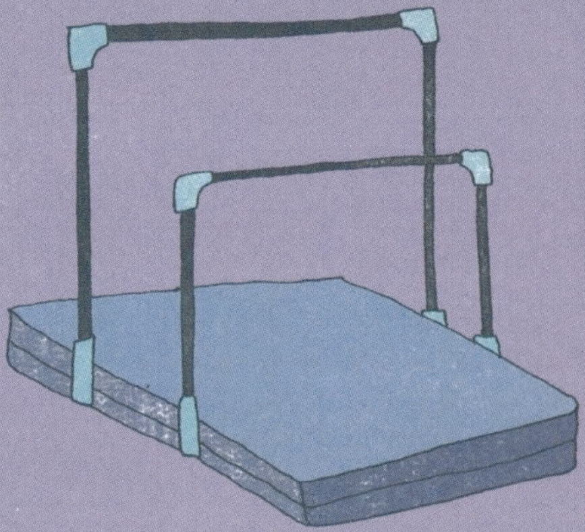

| | BAKING | GYMNASTICS | GAMING |
|---|---|---|---|
| PAULO | | | |
| NANCY | | | |
| HENRY | | | |

| | YOUTH CLUB | SCHOOL | HOME |
|---|---|---|---|
| PAULO | | | |
| NANCY | | | |
| HENRY | | | |

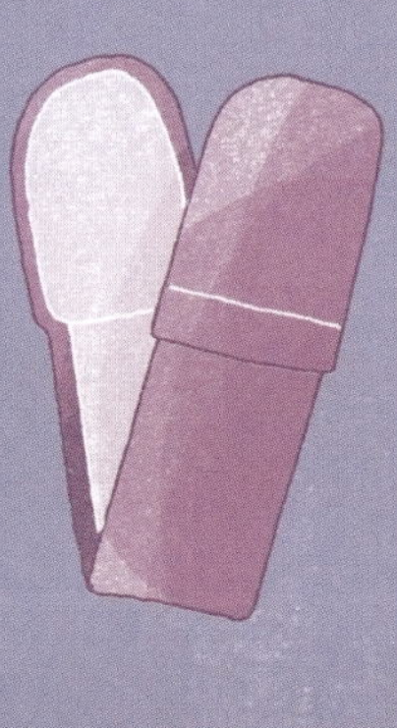

## Super-Power

Whenever we switch on a games console or light the oven, we are using energy. Where does that energy come from? Often, it involves burning fossil fuels, which is bad for the environment. We should all aim to use energy from renewable sources.

Find the house where the Eco family live:

It has solar panels on the roof.
A white electric car is parked outside.
It does not have a smoking chimney.

## Plugged In

Our homes use electricity to power washing machines, TVs, and fridges. These devices are often plugged in to a socket on the wall.

Which cable should Nico unplug now that his smart watch is fully charged?

# LIVING THINGS

Earth is the only planet in our Solar System that supports life. People are just one of the living things here; there are also plants, fungi, animals, and tiny single-celled things like amoebae, algae, and bacteria.

See if you can spot each of these creatures somewhere in the big picture. Which one is now extinct?

## Get Sorted

Scientists put living things into groups that share characteristics. The largest groups are kingdoms, such as plants, fungi, and animals. The smallest groups are species, such as blue whales and chimpanzees.

Use the clues to organize the groups from largest (at the top) to smallest (at the bottom).

| | |
|---|---|
| **species** is the lowest on the list | |
| **order** follows class but is above family | |
| **kingdom** is the very top category | |
| **family** is just above genus | |
| **phylum** comes immediately after kingdom | |
| **class** is four steps higher than species | |
| **genus** is second lowest on the list | |

## Match the Mushrooms

Living things that are part of the same species look similar to each other, and are able to reproduce.

Match these mushrooms and find one that's on its own.

# CELLS AND DNA

Cells are the building blocks of all organisms (living things). Different organisms consist of different types of cell. Some have only one type but most living things have many types, each with an important function.

The human body contains hundreds of types of cells but some are more common than others. This page shows six types of cell. Most of the cells are shown four times, but one cell is shown five times. Can you see which it is?

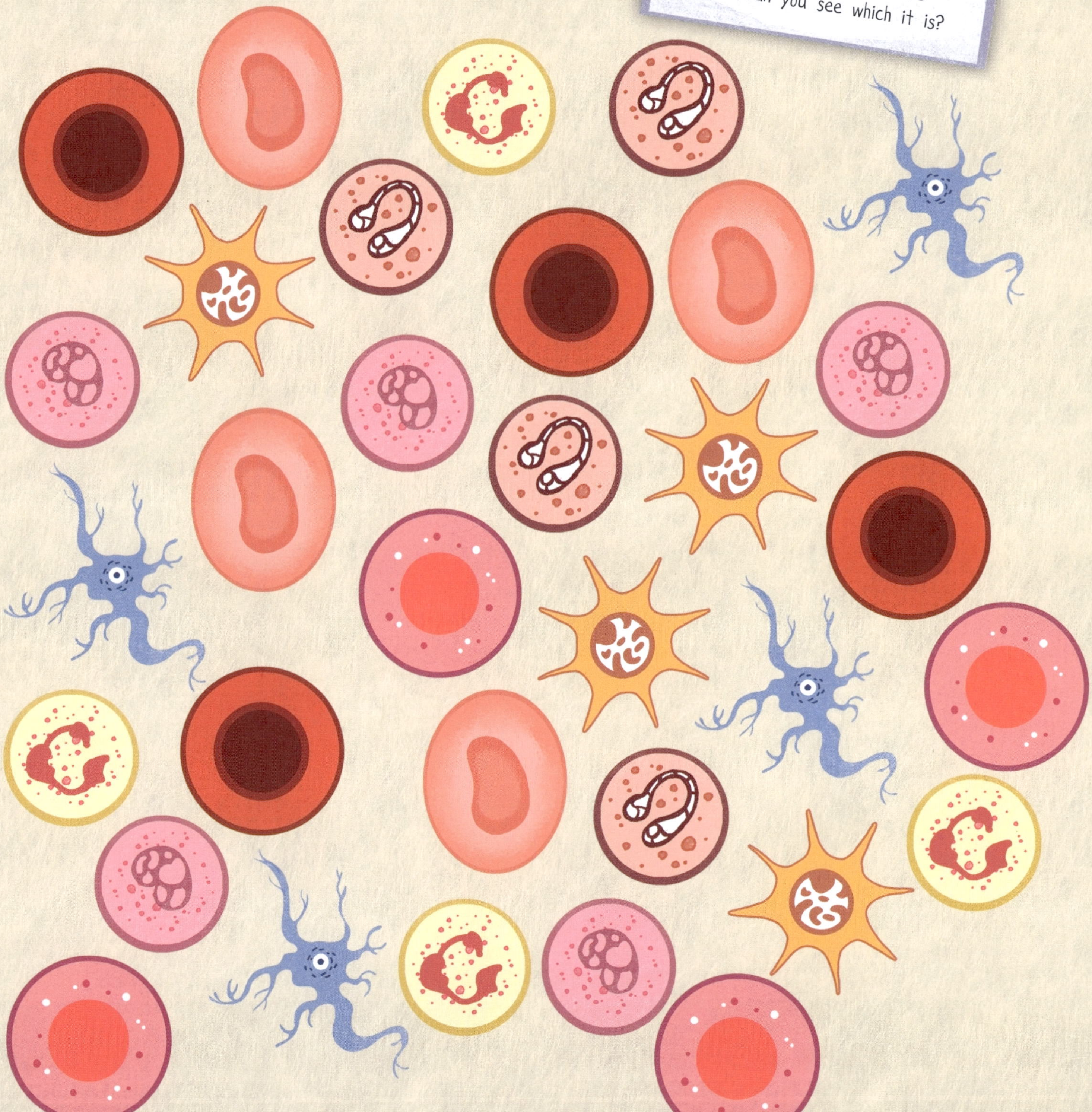

## Make Something New

The characteristics of a living thing are controlled by its genes, which are made of a chemical substance called deoxyribonucleic acid, or DNA. How many new words can you make from the letters in that name?

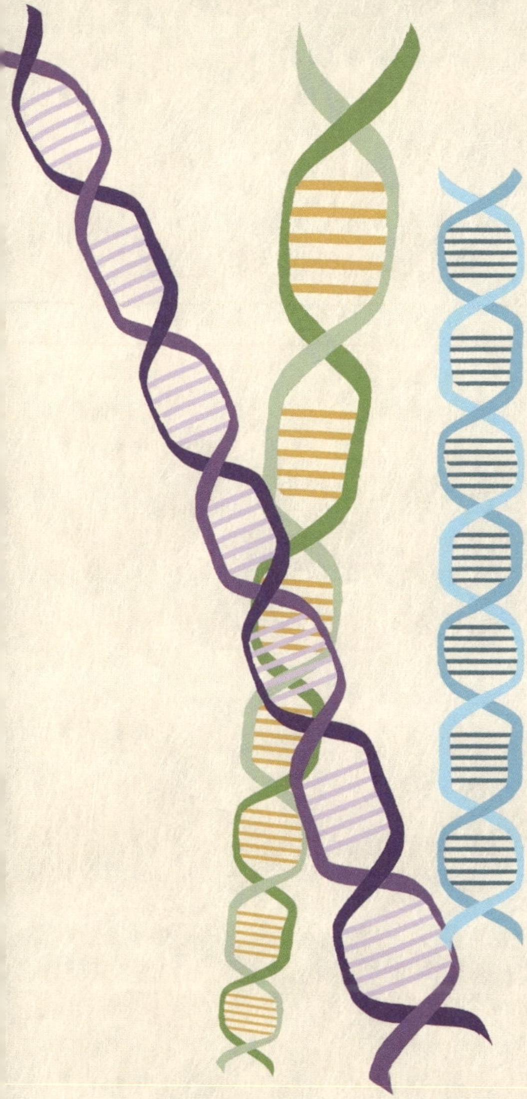

**DEOXYRIBONUCLEIC**

........................................ ........................................

........................................

........................................ ........................................

........................................

## In Their Genes

These hyenas all look very similar because most of their genes are identical. The few differences are down to slight genetic variations.

Find one that doesn't have an identical twin.

Animals kept in captivity can suffer from lack of genetic diversity. A global register of animals is used to match up breeding pairs for the best possible genetic health.

# TYPES OF TREE

There are two main groups of trees. Deciduous trees lose their leaves before winter, while evergreen trees keep their leaves all year round. Use all your shades of green for the trees at the top of the picture, and finish the trees at the bottom with red, orange, yellow, and brown.

Trees are among the oldest living things on Earth. They first appeared over 360 million years ago. Some trees that are still alive today are over 2,000 years old.

# Falling Leaves

Most deciduous trees are broadleaved, with wide, flat leaves in a variety of shapes. See how many different types you can find here. Don't be fooled by their different shades!

The weeping willow is one of the fastest-growing deciduous trees in the world. It can grow taller than a person in less than a year.

# Which is Which?

Look for all the trees in the grid. Those listed on the left are deciduous, while those on the right are evergreen.

OAK
MAPLE
BIRCH
POPLAR
ASH
WILLOW

| | | | | | | | | | | | |
|---|---|---|---|---|---|---|---|---|---|---|---|
| F | M | A | P | O | F | I | R | A | J | R | O |
| S | A | G | C | E | D | O | Q | O | Q | U | L |
| P | P | I | N | E | H | L | U | L | B | S | I |
| R | O | L | M | I | N | L | R | I | K | P | R |
| V | P | C | E | D | A | R | K | V | C | R | C |
| E | L | O | W | I | L | L | O | E | V | U | H |
| R | A | L | P | Q | A | S | H | O | S | C | D |
| B | R | L | H | H | E | L | T | T | E | E | T |
| O | F | Y | A | O | M | M | A | P | L | E | I |
| A | N | W | I | L | L | O | W | C | V | S | N |
| K | P | O | P | L | E | S | P | R | O | I | P |
| O | U | T | J | Y | T | B | I | R | C | H | I |

CEDAR
FIR
PINE
HOLLY
OLIVE
SPRUCE

# PARTS OF A PLANT

Each part of a plant has an important job to do. The three main parts of a plant are the roots, stem, and leaves, but they can look quite different from plant to plant. The roots are usually under the ground, and carry nutrients and water up to the plant.

The leaves contain a green substance called chlorophyll which absorbs light energy to make photosynthesis happen.

Find a way through this tangled root maze to the surface.

## HEALTHY PLANTS

Photosynthesis takes place in the leaves of a plant. During photosynthesis, the chlorophyll converts carbon dioxide (from the air) and water into oxygen and glucose. The plant uses the glucose as food to grow and stay healthy.

| A | B | C | D | E | F | G | H | I |
|---|---|---|---|---|---|---|---|---|
| 5 | 6 | | | | | | 12 | |

| J | K | L | M | N | O | P | Q | R |
|---|---|---|---|---|---|---|---|---|
| | | | | | | | | |

| S | T | U | V | W | X | Y | Z |
|---|---|---|---|---|---|---|---|
| 23 | | | | | | | |

Complete the key on the left then use the code to discover the world's fastest-growing plant.

| 6 | 5 | 17 | 6 | 19 | 19 |
|---|---|---|---|---|---|
| | | | | | |

# A Prickly Problem

Some plants, such as cactus plants, have modified leaves. These take the form of spines, which not only protect the plant, but prevent water loss in the desert and collect moisture from early morning fog and dew.

There are hundreds and hundreds of different types of cactus plant, in a wide range of shapes and sizes.

Which of these cactus plants has a shadow that doesn't exactly match?

# A PLANT'S LIFE CYCLE

All flowering plants go through a cycle of growing and reproducing (see page 36). A seed begins to grow and puts down roots to support it. The stem helps push it toward the light. It grows leaves to absorb sunlight. The flowers appear, to help move pollen between plants. The pollinated flowers produce seeds, and the cycle begins again.

Plants provide us with food to eat, and with oxygen to breathe. Join the dots to finish the missing parts of the plant life cycle.

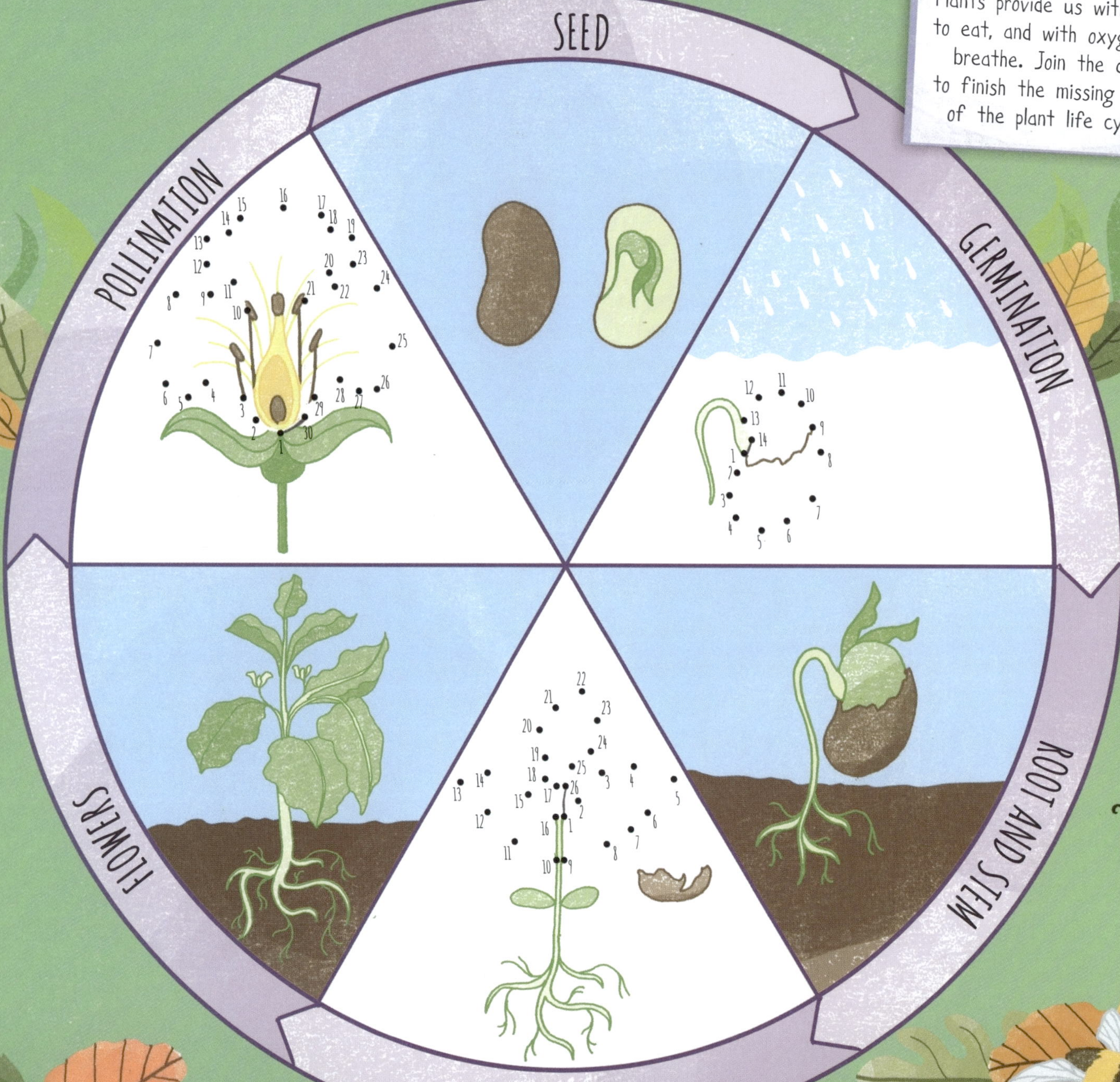

## How Does Your Garden Grow?

To grow successfully, a plant needs water, sunlight, air, the right temperature, and time. Without enough sunlight or water, its roots may be too weak and the plant will wither and die. They also gather nutrients from the soil to help them grow healthy and strong.

Draw some more gorgeous plants here!

## Watch Out!

Some plants trap animals, especially insects, and digest them to get the nutrition they need.

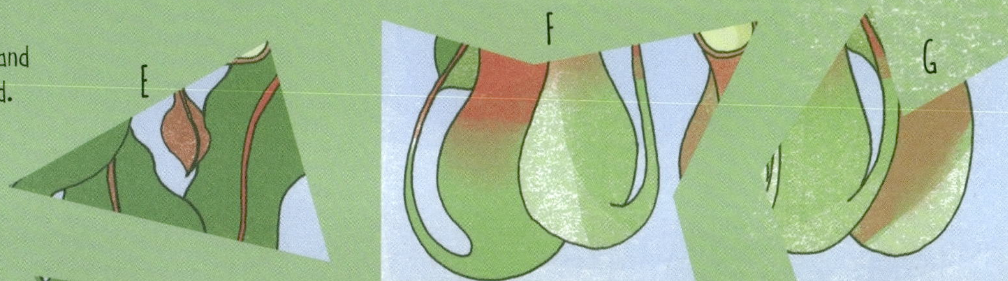


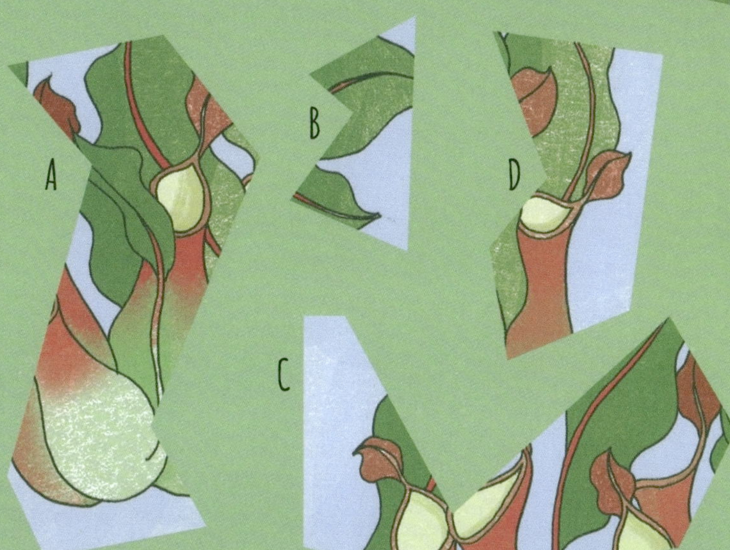


Which piece does not belong to this picture of a pitcher plant?

# REPRODUCTION IN PLANTS

Many plants have to spread their pollen in order to reproduce. Pollen can be carried by water or the wind, or moved around by creatures called pollinators. Bees, butterflies, and moths are well-known pollinators but pollen also gets carried from flower to flower by beetles, flies, wasps, mosquitoes, and even bats and birds.

START

FINISH

Help this bee get back to its nest, as quickly as it can.

Pollen grains stick to a bumblebee's furry body then it combs them off into little baskets on its legs.

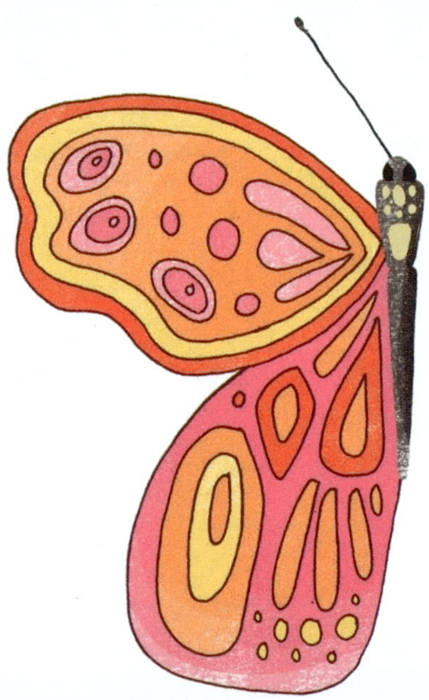

Draw the rest of this beautiful butterfly.

## Perfect Pollinator

Butterflies are attracted to flowers with bright petals and strong scents.

# Find a Friend

Many of our foods rely on pollination by insects and animals. Apples, berries, tomatoes, and nuts are pollinated by bees and other creatures. Even our dairy and meat farmers need pollination for the food crops that their animals feed on.

Count how many of the listed creatures you can see in this scene.

# ANIMAL GROUPS

Animals can be divided into vertebrates and invertebrates depending on whether they have a backbone (spine) or not. Invertebrates are easily the biggest group, making up around 97 percent of all living creatures.

Land invertebrates include worms, spiders, slugs, snails, and all insects. Others are found in the ocean, such as octopuses, jellyfish, sea stars, crabs, oysters, sponges, and corals.

Finish this picture of common invertebrates.

# LEAPING LEMURS!

Lemurs are part of the group of animals known as mammals. They live on the island of Madagascar, off the east coast of Africa.

Find two lemurs here that match each other exactly.

Mammals are one of the smallest, least diverse animal groups with only around 5,000 different species. Compare that to 10,000 bird species, 10,000 reptiles, and over 30,000 species of fish.

# MIX AND MATCH

Can you work out which of these animals are mammals, birds, reptiles, amphibians or fish? Follow the lines to find out.

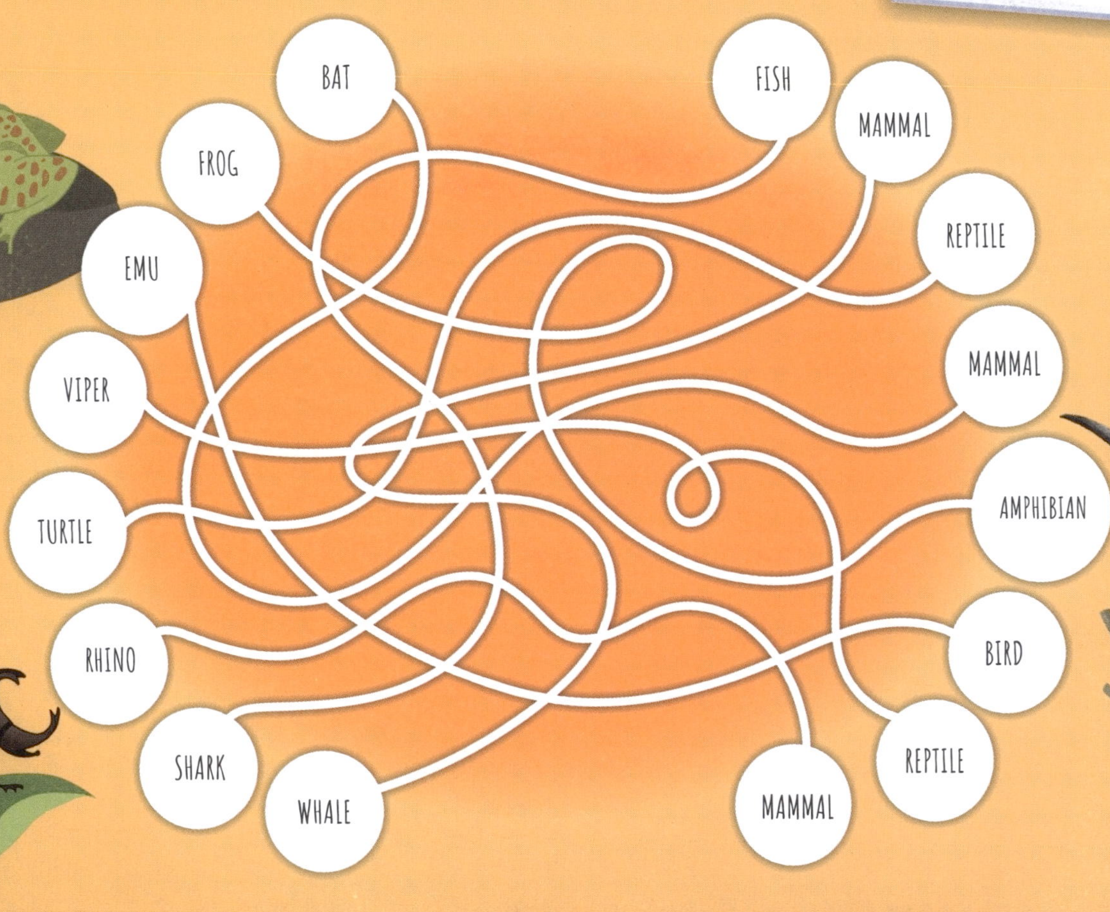

# MICROORGANISMS

Some living things are too tiny to see without a microscope. These microorganisms include algae, bacteria, protozoa, and tiny, tiny animals like dust mites and zooplankton.

Zooplankton are tiny sea creatures that cannot swim but drift in the ocean current. Some plankton are plants, not animals, and are called phytoplankton. Both are vitally important for the marine food chain.

Look at the plankton below. Can you find each one within the yellow oval? Circle each one when you find it.

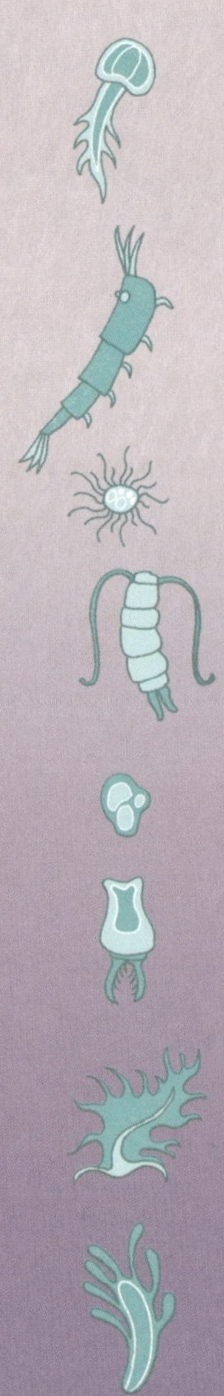

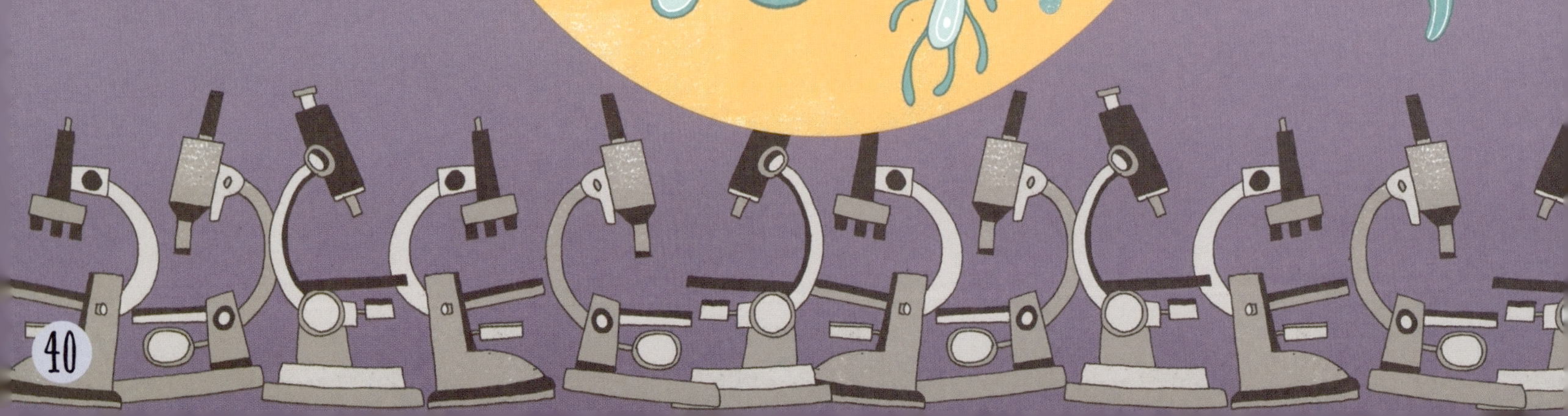

# A Closer Look

A high-powered single lens microscope was invented in the 1670s by Dutch scientist Antonie van Leeuwenhoek. He used it to study yeast, red blood cells, mouth bacteria, and protozoa. At the same time, English scientist Robert Hooke was observing all kinds of things under his own microscope.

Can you find seven differences between these two pictures of magnified fleas?

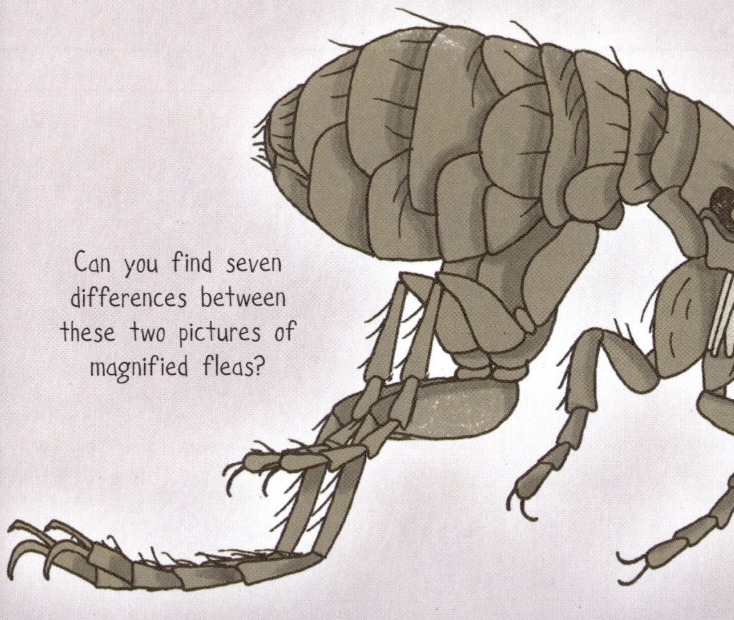

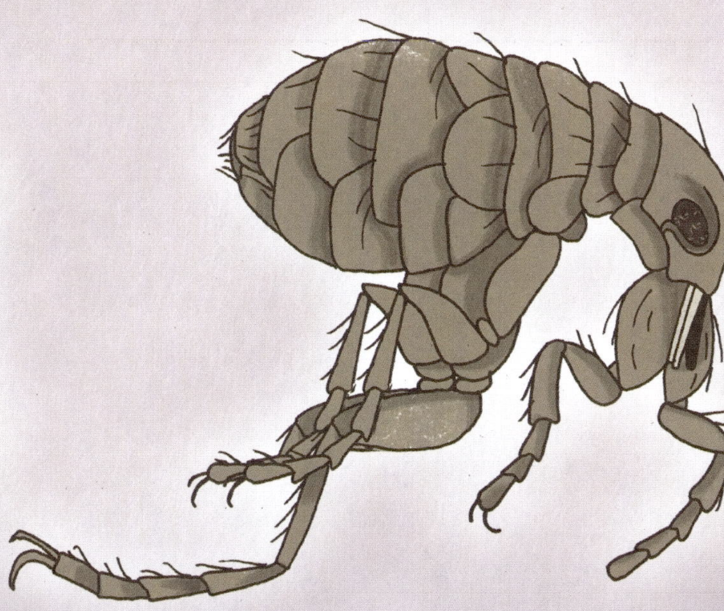

# On the Rise

Yeast is a type of microorganism. It is helpful as it makes bread rise.

Use the clues to work out which type of bread is the most popular in the bakery today.

IT'S A LOAF, NOT SMALL ROLLS.

IT IS NOT A PLAITED LOAF.

THE LONG, THIN BAGUETTES ARE NOT POPULAR TODAY.

IT'S NOT A LOAF WITH LOTS OF SEEDS ON IT.

THE LOAF CANNOT BE CUT INTO RECTANGULAR SLICES.

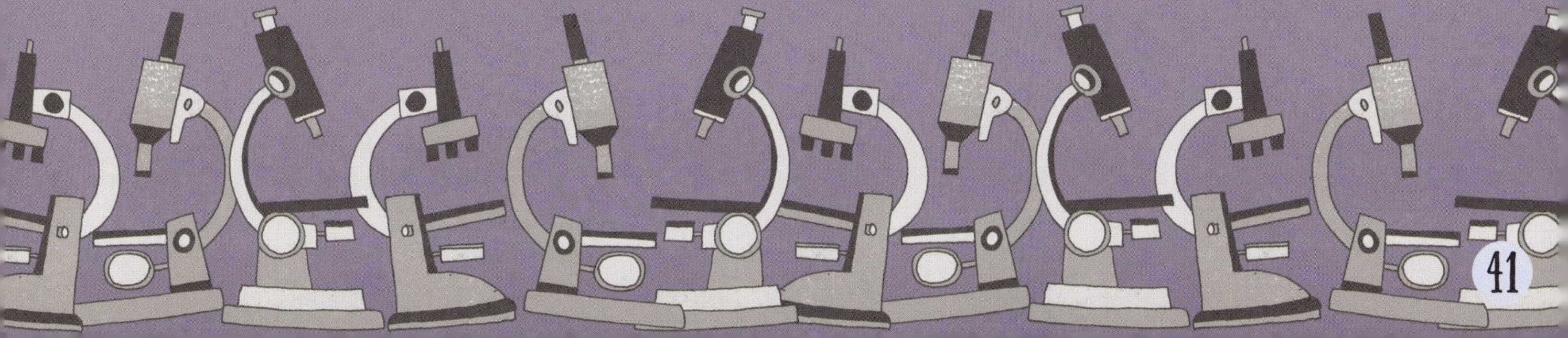

# WHAT ANIMALS EAT

Animals can be put into categories based on their physical characteristics, but also based on what they eat.

Match the animal diet with its description by writing the correct letter after each sentence. Then write a number next to each animal to show its diet.

A. insectivore

B carnivore

C. herbivore

D. frugivore

E. omnivore

1. An animal that eats mainly fruit ___
2. An animal that eats mostly plants ___
3. An animal that eats mainly insects ___
4. An animal that eats other animals ___
5. An animal that eats all kinds of things ___

# Gentle Giant

Gorillas may be enormous, with huge teeth and powerful limbs, but they are gentle plant-eaters that spend hours munching on stems, shoots, and fruits.

Choose the missing pieces to complete the picture of this majestic silverback male.

A

B

C

D

E

F

# Mighty Meat-eater

Join the dots to find one of the planet's biggest, strongest, most awe-inspiring carnivores. These creatures spend half their time hunting, can weigh as much as ten men, and have an exceptional sense of smell for sniffing out distant prey.

What is the animal called?

______________________________

# ANIMAL HABITATS

Animals adapt to live in a variety of places, from hot deserts to tropical rain forests. Find two animals to go in each of these habitats.

Mountain animals have to cope with rocky ground.

ibex

cheetah

arctic fox

America's grasslands are known as prairies.

prairie dog

Many forest animals sleep during the winter.

snow leopard

beaver

The savanna is Africa's tropical grassland.

proboscis monkey

Rain forests are home to a richer variety of animals than other habitats.

Tundra soil is frozen for much of the year.

orangutan

ostrich

bear

bison

reindeer

# Hot, Hot, Hot

Camels can survive the extremes of a hot desert. The one-humped dromedary is found in the Sahara Desert. These camels hardly sweat, can eat prickly desert plants, and store fat in their hump for when food is scarce.

Which of these silhouettes is not a true match to the camel here?

# ...And Very Cold

Animals live on every continent, even the icy Antarctic where temperatures drop to fifty degrees below zero.

Draw more emperor penguins here on the ice.

# ANIMALS AND PLANTS

Living things move, reproduce, sense things, grow, respire (breathe), excrete waste, and consume food. Non-living things may do some of these things—but never all seven! Some things—like our food, wooden furniture, or cotton clothes—were once alive but are now non-living.

Fill in a letter code for these pictures.
A = are alive, O = were once alive, N = have never lived

# What a Waste

Living things get rid of waste in a process known as excretion. Animals excrete waste by breathing out, vomiting, and peeing and pooping.

Organize these six pieces of pipe to make this toilet capable of flushing properly.

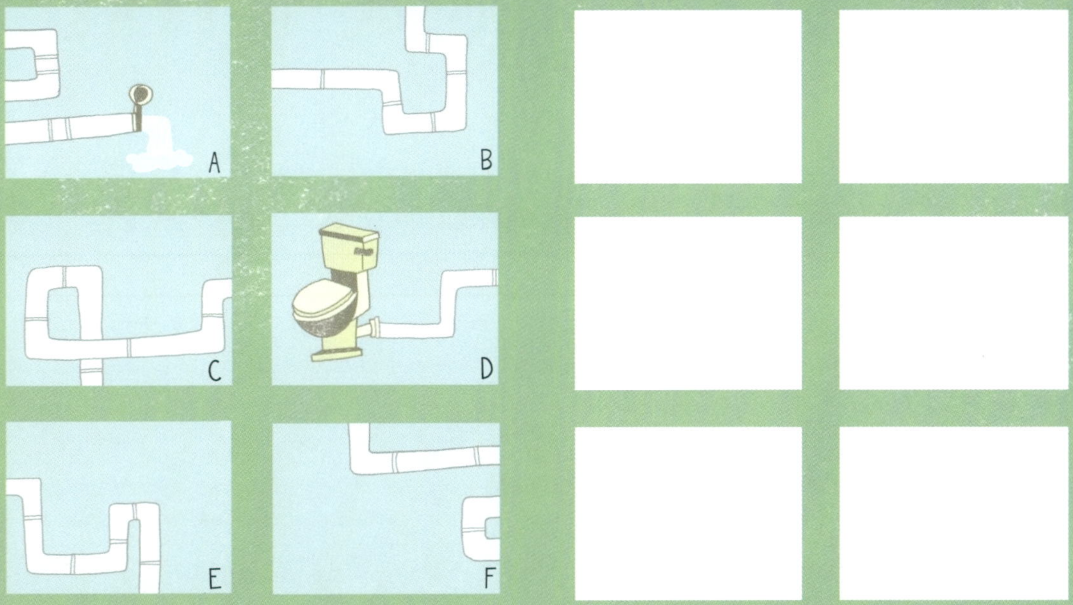


Even plants excrete—they expel waste gases through their leaves.

# On the Move

Living things move by themselves (without being pushed or pulled or driven by an engine).

Look at these two scenes to find seven things that have moved.

# FOOD CHAINS

Most plants make their own food; animals eat plants; other animals eat those animals. This is how living things get their energy, and is known as a food chain.

Look at the living things on this page and guess which category they belong to:
1 = Producer (makes its own food)
2 = Primary consumer (eats plants)
3 = Secondary consumer (eats plants and/or insects and small animals)
4 = Apex predator (eats animals, and has no natural predators of its own)

# Food Webs

Living things usually eat more than one type of food. This means that most food chains are interlinked into a food web.

Unscramble the letters to write the correct labels into this food web.

Not all predators are large, and not all primary consumers are small! Elephants, rhinos, and hippos eat only plants but are the biggest land animals on Earth.

# All at Sea

Ocean food chains are all about the Fs: lots of fish, and top predators that are finned, flippered, or feathered. They nearly all begin with phytoplankton, tiny one-celled organisms that provide food for thousands of different ocean creatures.

Find these creatures in the grid:

| FEATHERED | FINNED | FLIPPERED |
|---|---|---|
| pelican | shark | seal |
| penguin | tuna | turtle |
| gull | orca | walrus |

# HUMAN BODY

The body is a clever machine made of lots of parts that work together in amazing ways. We can see our limbs, hair, and facial features, but the body also includes the parts inside us too, such as our skeleton and organs.

Add in the missing labels on the picture. Read the facts to help you.

LUNGS
LIVER
STOMACH
BLADDER
LARGE INTESTINE
SMALL INTESTINE

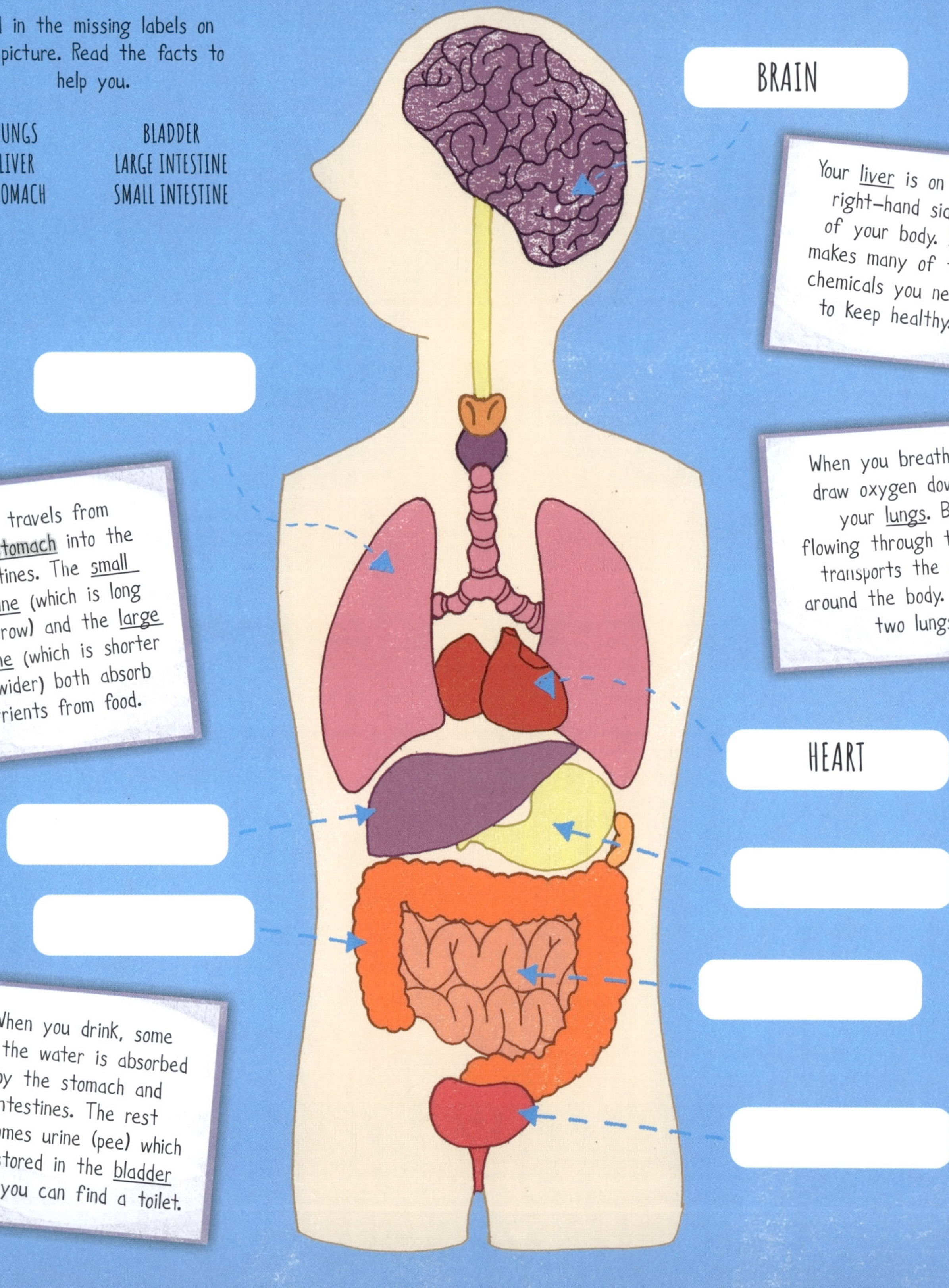


Your liver is on the right-hand side of your body. It makes many of the chemicals you need to keep healthy.

When you breathe, you draw oxygen down into your lungs. Blood flowing through the lungs transports the oxygen around the body. You have two lungs.

Food travels from your stomach into the intestines. The small intestine (which is long and narrow) and the large intestine (which is shorter and wider) both absorb nutrients from food.

When you drink, some of the water is absorbed by the stomach and intestines. The rest becomes urine (pee) which is stored in the bladder until you can find a toilet.

# BONY BITS

Our skeleton supports our body, protects our internal organs, and helps us to move around. We can look at the bones by taking an X-ray image.

Add up the numbers on these X-rays to find out how many bones are in the adult human body.

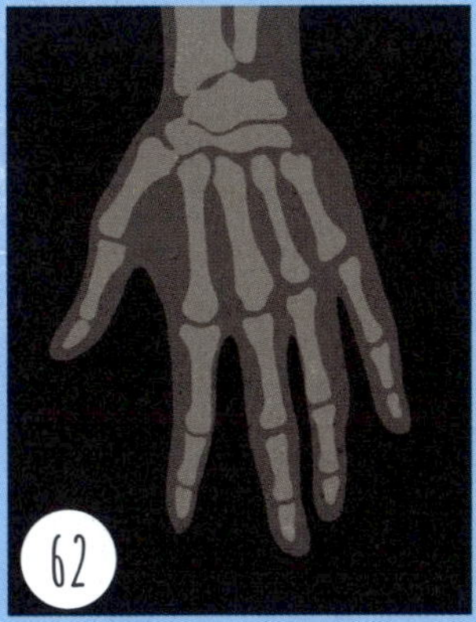


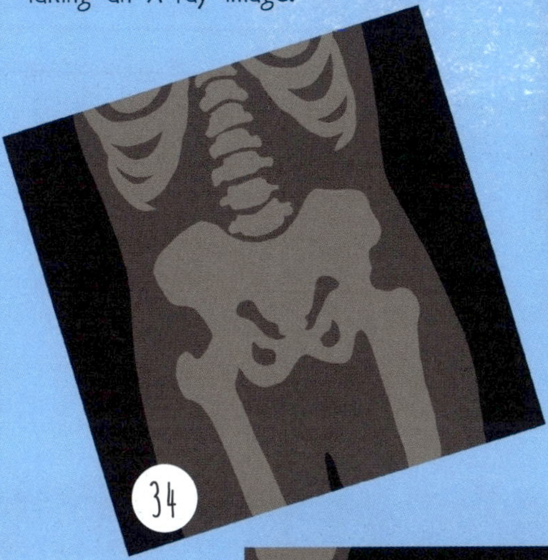


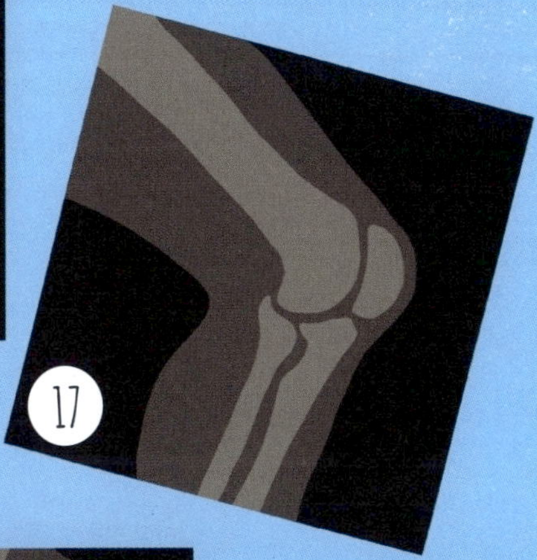


Over half of our bones are in our hands and feet.

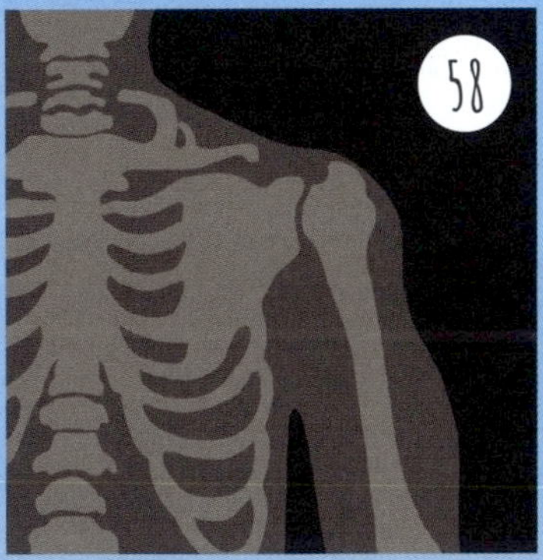


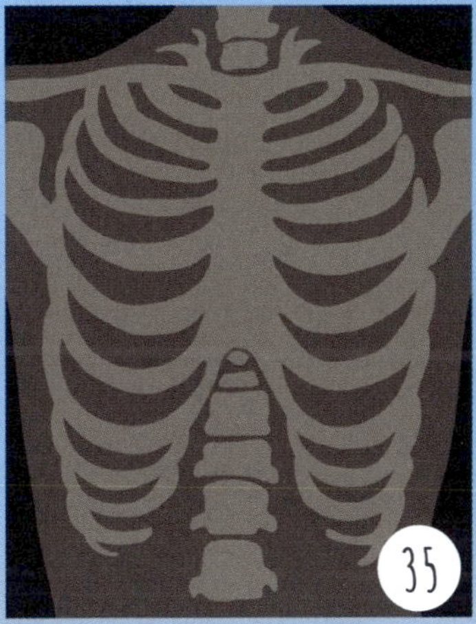


# HIGH FIVE

Fingernails, toenails, and hair are all made of a material called Keratin. Keratin is also found in your skin. It helps to make your body parts stronger and tougher.

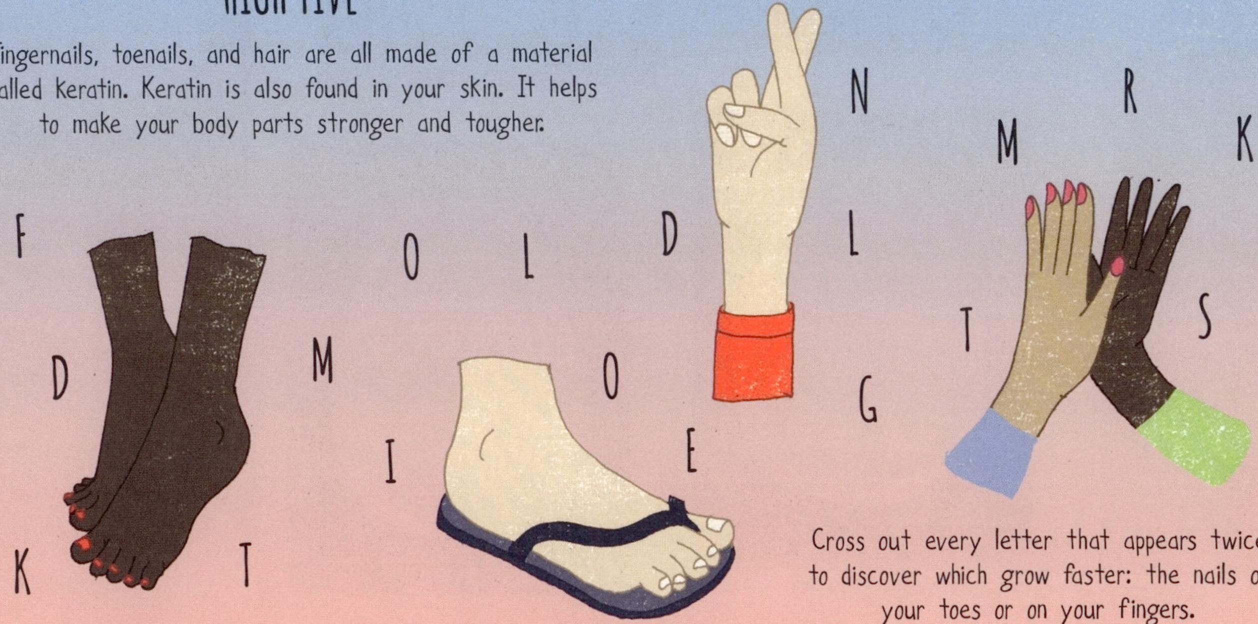


Cross out every letter that appears twice to discover which grow faster: the nails on your toes or on your fingers.

# HUMAN SENSES

The senses help the body pass on messages about the outside world to the brain. Receptors in different parts of the brain help to process these sensory messages. Scientists can take images of the brain and study which parts are activated.

A

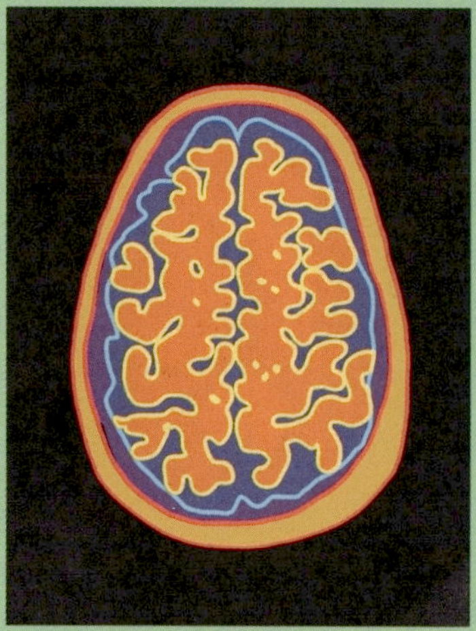

B

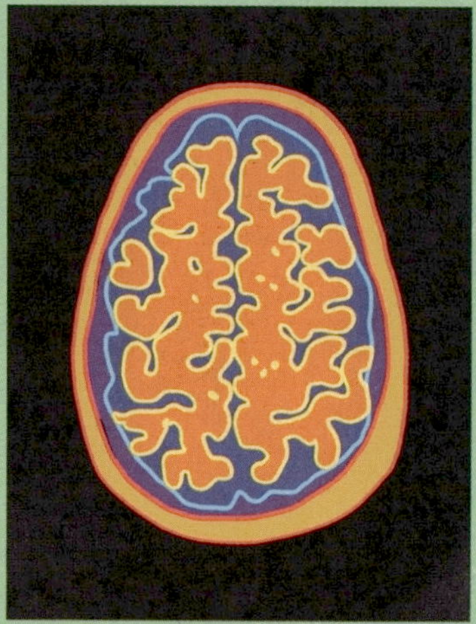

C

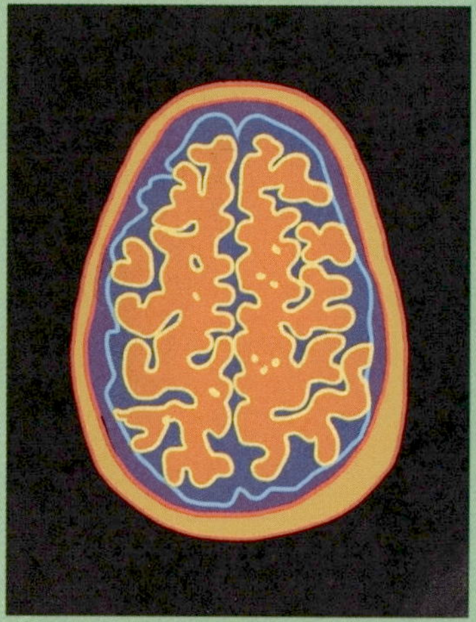

D

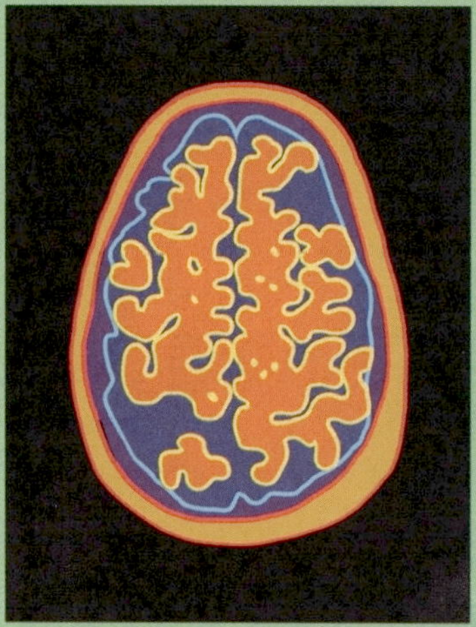

E

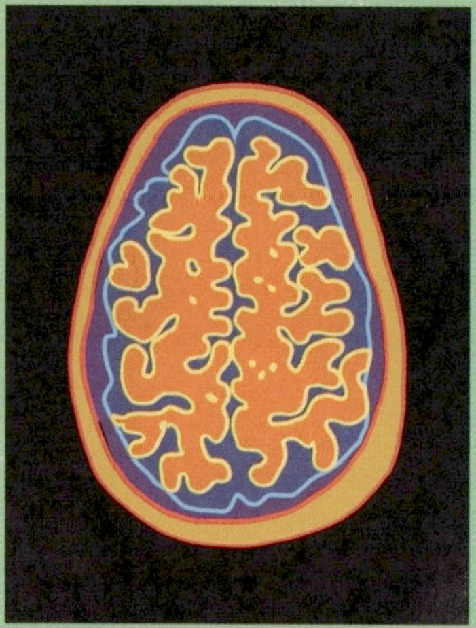

Which one of these scans is different from the others?

F

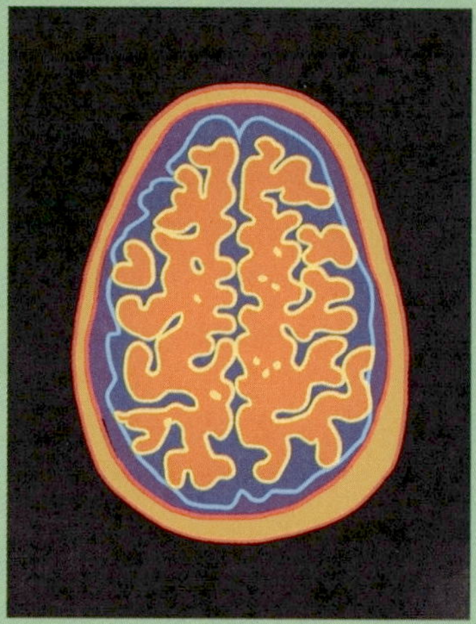

G

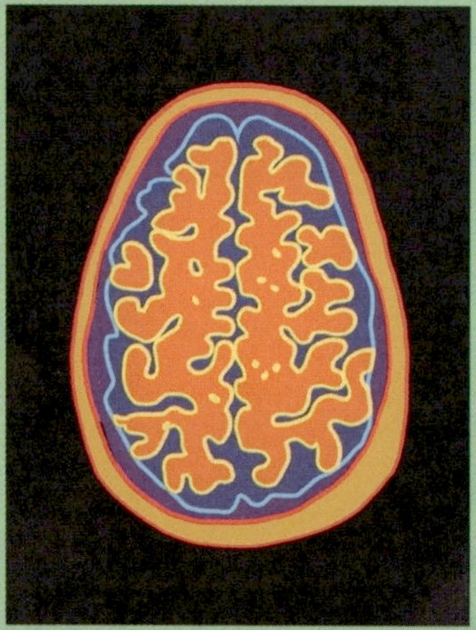

H

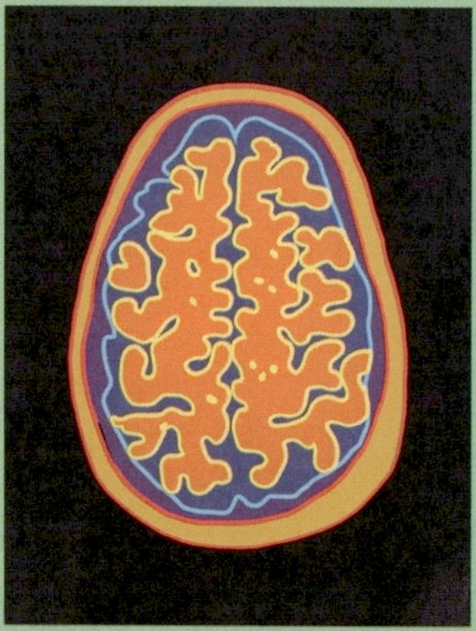

Some people have a condition called synesthesia. It makes their brain combine senses in unusual ways, such as tasting lemon when they hear the word "roof" or feeling a tap on the knee when they see a train.

## Brain Test

You have many different senses, but the best-known ones are sight, hearing, smell, taste, and touch. Fill in the grid so that each row, column, and minigrid contains each of the five senses plus the brain.

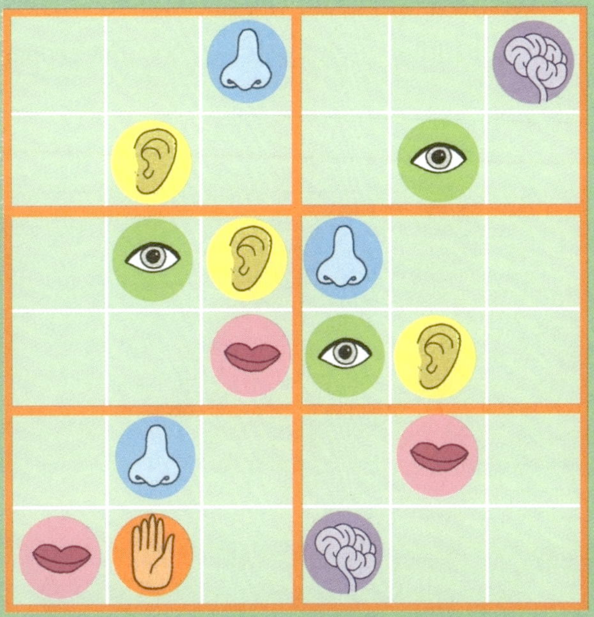

## Use Your Eyes

The eyes are the organ of sight. They take in information about shapes, patterns, directions, and movements.

Use your eyes and brain to solve this visual puzzle: How many squares are in this image? Count every one that you can see.

HINT: There are more than 30 squares.

# NUTRITION

We need to eat a balanced diet to fuel our body, grow and heal, and generally stay healthy. That means eating the proper amount from different food groups.

Unscramble the letters to spell out some different types of nutrients that the body needs.

A good way to be sure you're getting a whole mix of vitamins and minerals is to eat a rainbow of vegetables and fruits every week. Dark green and orange vegetables are especially good for you.

# A Good Start

Eating a healthy breakfast can help you get enough from all the food groups. It helps your brain work better, too, allowing you to focus and remember things.

Cover the second picture and study the first one for a minute. Now cover the first picture, and see if you can spot two items that have been eaten.

# Get Your Greens

It is vital that you eat enough vegetables every day. They provide a wide range of nutrients, are low in calories, keep you feeling full, and help your digestive system to function well.

Work out how much each vegetable is worth in this table.

# SEASONS OF THE YEAR

In many countries, the year consists of four seasons. The weather is generally hot in the summer and cold in the winter.

The seasons are caused by the tilt of the Earth. It makes different parts of the Earth point toward the Sun so that they receive more direct rays. When the North Pole tilts toward the Sun, it is summer in the Northern Hemisphere.

1

Study the diagrams which show how the Earth orbits around the Sun in one year. Match the correct caption to each one.

2

March: Spring in the north. The Sun shines equally on both hemispheres.

December: Summer in the south. The Sun shines directly on the Southern Hemisphere.

3

June: Summer in the north. The Sun shines directly on the Northern Hemisphere.

4

September: Spring in the south. The Sun shines equally on both hemispheres.

## Wet and Dry

Much of Africa has only two seasons, the rainy season and the dry season.

Circle every second letter to spell the name of two countries that experience a rainy season from around November to March.

## Bring on the Rain

Tropical areas, especially India and southeast Asia, have monsoons. The summer monsoon usually brings a humid climate and extremely heavy rains. Water from these rains help to drive hydroelectric power plants.

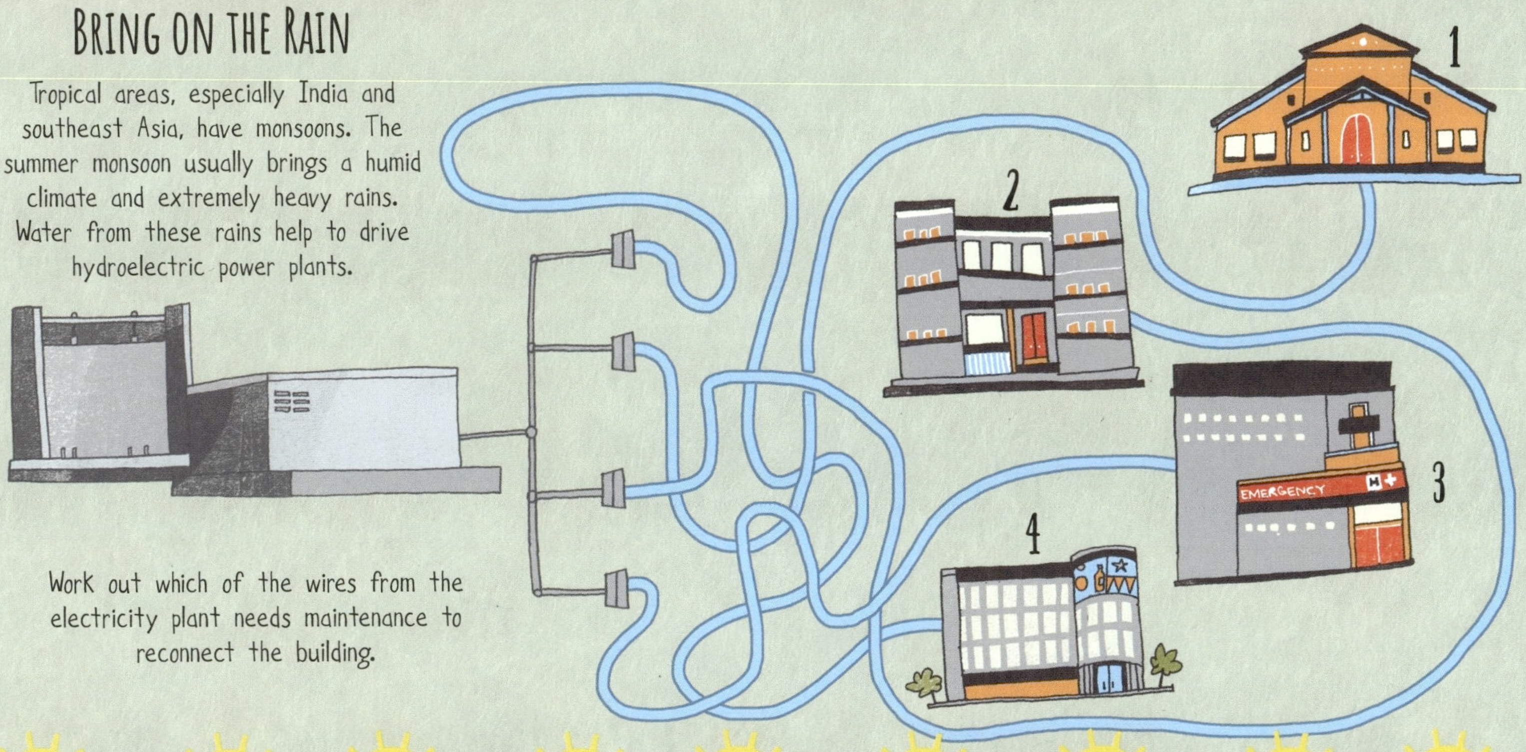


Work out which of the wires from the electricity plant needs maintenance to reconnect the building.

# WEATHER AND CLIMATE

It's easy to see what the weather is today; just look outside. The climate, however, is a pattern of weather for an area over a much longer period of time. Climate and the weather are controlled by a place's position on Earth, and by oceans and mountains. Some climate types are mostly dry, while others are hot and humid with lots of rain.

The world's wettest town is Mawsynram, but what country is it in? Splash through the puddles, circling those that contain multiples of 4. Use those letters to find out.

- B 11
- I 24
- E 3
- N 9
- P 22
- S 30
- Y 17
- S 18
- N 40
- D 16
- D 9
- M 21
- F 33
- A 45
- A 48
- I 36
- W 15
- C 19
- R 42
- H 13

# Whatever the Weather

Most of the weather on Earth occurs in a part of the planet's atmosphere called the troposphere. This is where clouds form, bringing rain, snow, and hail. Unscramble all of these weather words and write them in the correct place.

Around 2,000 thunderstorms happen every minute around the world.

DUYCOL _ _ _ _ _ _

NYNUS _ _ _ _ _

AGRININ _ _ _ _ _ _ _

DYNWI _ _ _ _ _

NOWSING _ _ _ _ _ _ _

STROSM _ _ _ _ _ _

# Let It Snow

The shape of a snowflake is affected by the temperature of the air around it.

Look carefully in this blizzard to find the three snowflakes shown here:

It takes about an hour for a snowflake to leave its cloud and fall to the ground.

# THE WATER CYCLE

Earth is a watery planet. Over 70 percent of its surface is covered in water in some form. The water cycle is the process where water is transferred between the surface and the atmosphere. Water is stored in the atmosphere as clouds and falls to Earth as rain, snow, sleet, and hail.

# Where the Water Is

Nearly 97 percent of the Earth's water is in the oceans. A small percentage is found in lakes, rivers, streams, and the ground, and another small percentage is frozen at the poles and in glaciers. Finish this scene, showing some of the creatures you might find in the ocean.

Over half of the oxygen we breathe is produced by the oceans.

The water on Earth regulates the planet's temperature. Without the water cycle, Earth would be either too hot or too cold.

The ocean is home to the planet's largest creature, the blue whale, and some of its smallest creatures too, such as microscopic plankton (see page 40).

Use the clues to work out the name of each player on the pink team.

KIT IS TWO PLACES BEHIND ROWAN.

ROWAN IS IN FRONT OF TJ.

MORGAN IS AT THE FRONT.

# FORCES

Forces make things move, speed up, slow down, change direction, stop, or even change shape. When you pull hard in a tug-of-war, that's a force. The push you feel when holding down a spring is also a force. And when you cycle down a hill and feel the wind pushing against you, that's a force too! Forces are everywhere.

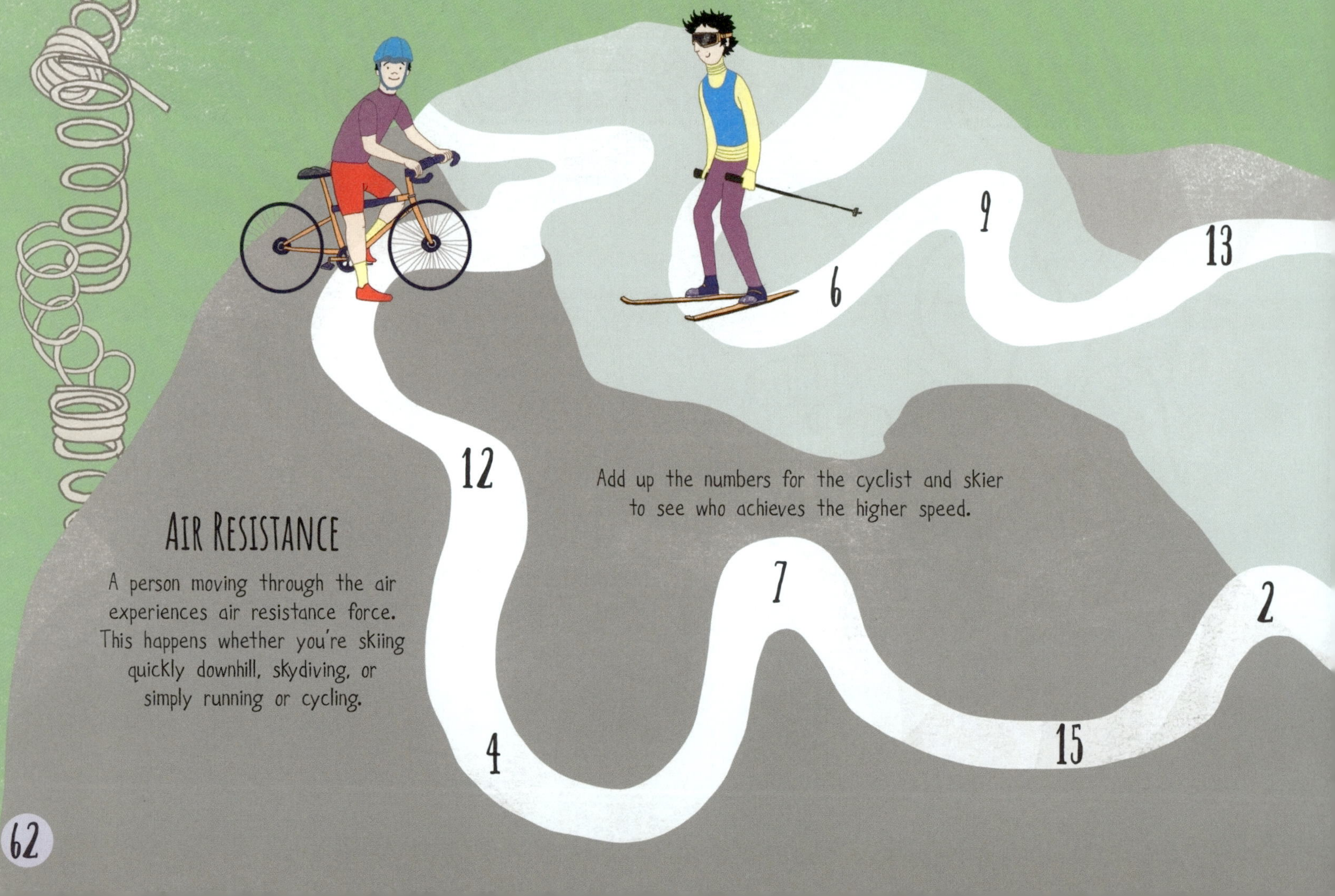


Add up the numbers for the cyclist and skier to see who achieves the higher speed.

## AIR RESISTANCE

A person moving through the air experiences air resistance force. This happens whether you're skiing quickly downhill, skydiving, or simply running or cycling.

In a tug-of-war, if both teams pull with equal force, the rope will not move. One team has to exert a greater force to win. Pulling on a rope is a tension force, a type of applied force. Other examples of applied force are twisting the lid on a bottle to open it, kicking a ball, pushing a glass to move it away from the edge of a table, and pulling a door closed behind you.

BOING!

Spring force is created when an external force causes a spring to change its shape. When the force is removed, the spring goes back to its original shape.

How many springs are shown here?

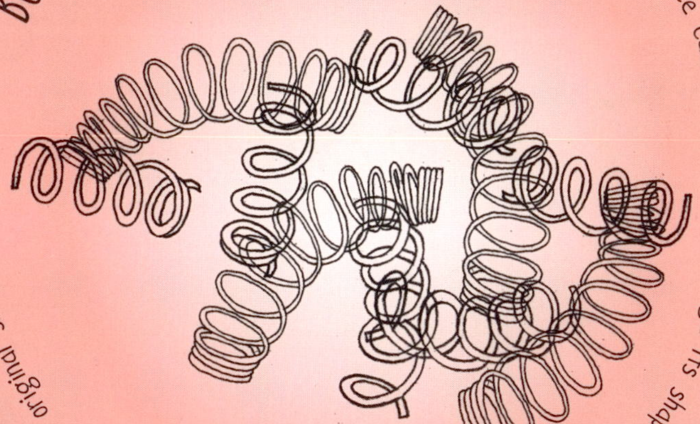

You can see spring force in action in a bungee jump, an elastic band, a bow firing an arrow, a trampoline, and even when you press the keys on a computer keyboard.

# MAGNETS

Magnetism is a force that affects some metals, pushing or pulling them from a distance. The main magnetic metal is iron. Steel (used in cars and some drinks cans) is an alloy made of carbon and lots of iron, so is also magnetic. Most metals, including gold and silver, are non-magnetic. All non-metals are not magnetic.

Circle the only magnetic item in each of these rows of items.

You can test how strong a magnet is by seeing how many paperclips it will hold.

# Poles Apart

The Earth's core is mostly made of iron, making the Earth act like a giant magnet. Earth's poles correspond to the poles on a small magnet. This is why the needle on a compass always points north.

Can you spot six small differences between these compasses?

A magnet has two poles, north and south. Opposite poles pull together but like poles push each other away.

## Show Me the Way

A compass can help you decide which direction you should take.

Start on a red arrow and move the number of squares it shows. Only one route leads to the blue circle; which one is it?

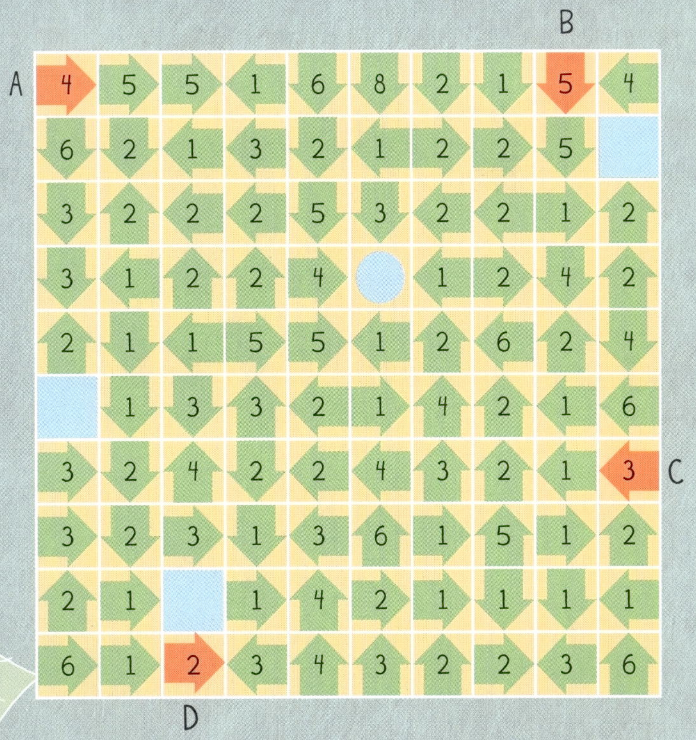

# GRAVITY

The force of gravity is at work on a large scale, keeping the planets in orbit around the Sun, and on a smaller scale, here on Earth. It is gravity that keeps our feet on the ground and stops all our belongings flying off into space.

Look at these facts and put an N next to the ones that are about Newton, and an E next to the ones about Einstein. Read the fact boxes for clues!

Gravity was first properly described by the English scientist Isaac Newton in 1687. His work was improved upon by Einstein in 1915. Einstein's theories of relativity helped scientists understand light, energy, mass, and time.

HIS FIRST NAME WAS ISAAC.

HE WAS BORN IN ENGLAND IN 1642.

HE IS FAMOUS FOR HIS THEORIES OF RELATIVITY.

HIS FIRST NAME WAS ALBERT.

The first of Newton's laws of motion states that an object stays at rest—or, if moving, continues to move—unless acted upon by a force.

HE IS CONSIDERED TO BE THE MOST INFLUENTIAL PHYSICIST OF THE 20TH CENTURY.

HE IS FAMOUS FOR HIS THREE LAWS OF MOTION.

HE WAS BORN IN GERMANY IN 1879.

# G-FORCE

When you stand still, Earth's gravity exerts 1 g of force on your body. If you ride a roller coaster, take off in a plane, or brake really hard in a fast car, this g-force increases and you can feel it.

Find these close-ups in the big picture.

## PLANETARY PULL

Objects with more mass have more gravity. If you were able to land on other planets, your mass, and therefore your weight, would change according to the size (mass) of that planet. Follow the lines to work out how much a 45 kg (100 lb) person would weigh on other planets.

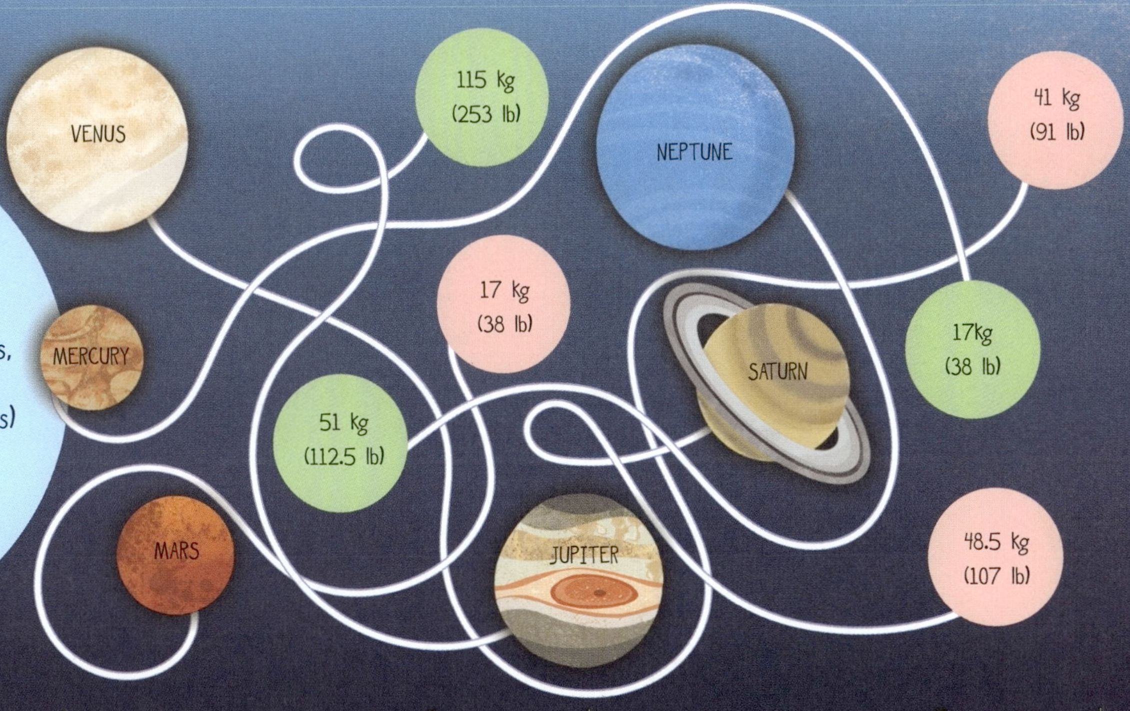

# FRICTION

Friction is a force between two surfaces that are trying to slide across each other. Friction slows down moving objects.

Can you find each of these people in this slippery scene?

Ice causes much less friction than many other surfaces. That's why it's easy to skate and sled, but also easy to slip over when you walk.

## Get a Grip!

The pattern on the soles of your shoes is called the tread. It is designed to increase friction so that you don't slip. Match the tread patterns into pairs, and find one that is on its own.

## Space Travel

There is no friction pushing back against objects in space, so a rocket can travel at a constant speed, even with its engines off.

In the vacuum of space, there aren't enough particles to create friction.

Add the numbers on each rocket to find which has moved the greatest distance on its travels.

# ELECTRICITY

Electricity is the flow of electrons from one place to another. We have only used it as an energy source in homes since the late 19th century. It can be stored in a battery or carried through wires around a circuit in your home.

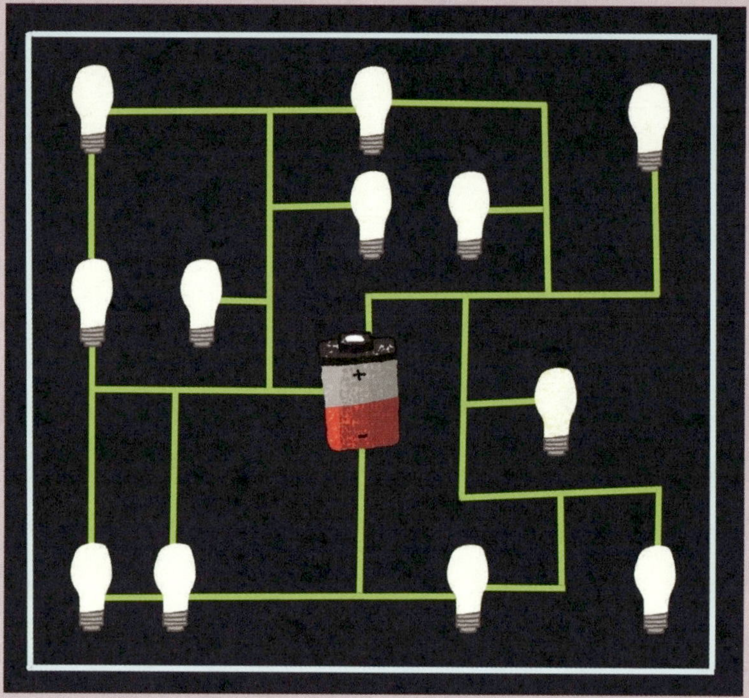

To light up a bulb, electricity must flow in a circuit which means it must be connected to both the positive and negative parts of a battery.

Use a yellow pen to shade in the bulbs that will light up on these two diagrams.

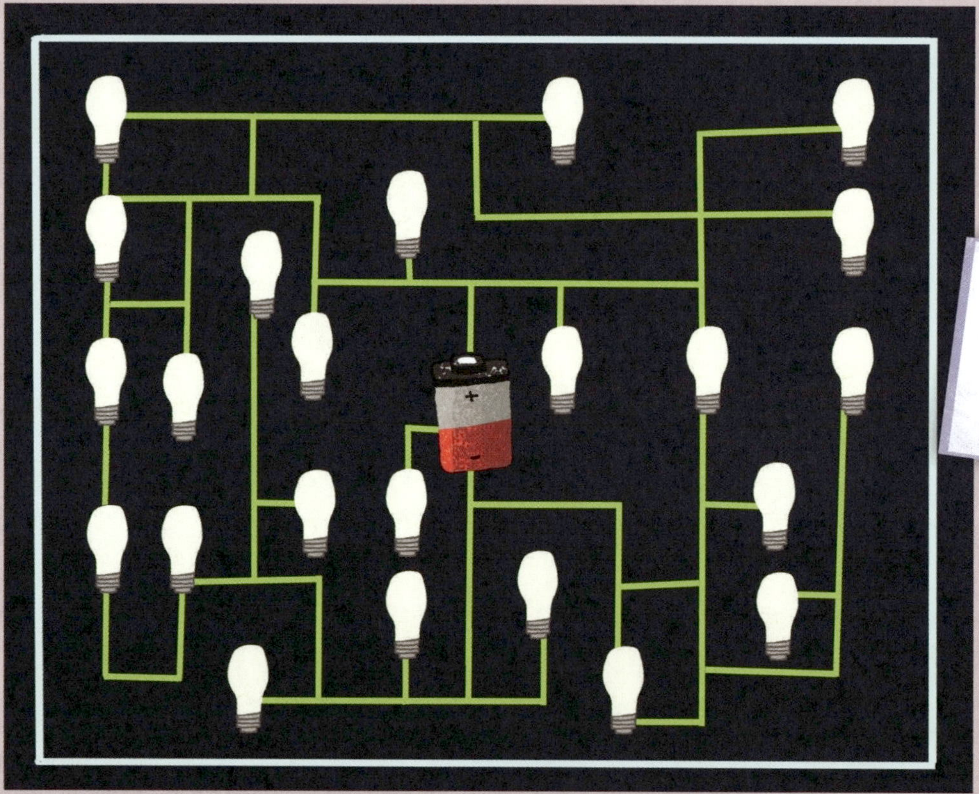

Sometimes, electricity doesn't flow, but builds up in one place. This is called static electricity.

## Electric Forces

Like magnetism and gravity, electrostatic force is a non-contact force. Particles carry positive or negative charges which can repel or attract. These charges build up in storm clouds, creating lightning.

Lake Maracaibo is the most lightning-struck place in the world, with as many as 40,000 strikes per night for up to 300 nights per year! Circle every second letter to find out which country it is in.

## On the Move

Electric motors are found in all kinds of things, from remote controlled cars and computer fans to hairdryers and microwaves.

Guide the remote control car around these paths. At each corner or junction the car can either turn right or go straight on—no left turns allowed!

# MOTION

Motion is the study of how things move. Around 300 years ago, Isaac Newton proposed that all things move according to three basic laws. They help us to understand how objects behave when they are still, when they are moving, and when forces act on them.

$$\Rightarrow f \propto \frac{mv - mu}{t}$$

$$\Rightarrow f \propto ma$$

$$\Rightarrow f = kma$$

$$F = ma$$

$$\Rightarrow f \propto \frac{m(v-u)}{t}$$

$$f \propto \frac{dP}{dt}$$

Newton's third law is well-known. It states that when two objects interact, they exert equal and opposite forces on each other. So, if Kate and Nate are both wearing skates, and Kate pushes Nate, they will both roll off in opposite directions, at a similar speed and for a similar distance.

Help Phoebe skate her way through the maze to join Tom.

# The First Law

Newton's first law is simple. It states that an object remains in the same state of motion unless a force acts on it. So a stationary object stays still, and a moving object stays moving (at the same speed and in the same direction) unless you push it, stop it, or a force such as gravity or friction acts on it.

Newton's first law is often known by another name. Solve the code to find out what it is.

| A | B | C | D | E | F | G | H | I |
|---|---|---|---|---|---|---|---|---|
| 1 | 2 | | | | | | | |

| J | K | L | M | N | O | P | Q | R |
|---|---|---|---|---|---|---|---|---|
| | 11 | | | | | | | |

| S | T | U | V | W | X | Y | Z |
|---|---|---|---|---|---|---|---|
| 19 | | | | | | | |

12.1.23 / 15.6 / 9.14.5.18.20.9.1

_ _ _ / _ _ /

_ _ _ _ _ _ _ _

$$\Rightarrow f \propto \frac{mv - mu}{t}$$

$$\Rightarrow f \propto ma$$

$$\Rightarrow f = kma$$

$$F = ma$$

$$\Rightarrow f \propto \frac{m(v-u)}{t}$$

$$f \propto \frac{dP}{dt}$$

$$\Rightarrow f \propto ma$$

$$\Rightarrow f = kma$$

$$F = ma$$

$$\Rightarrow f \propto \frac{m(v-u)}{t}$$

$$f \propto \frac{dP}{dt}$$

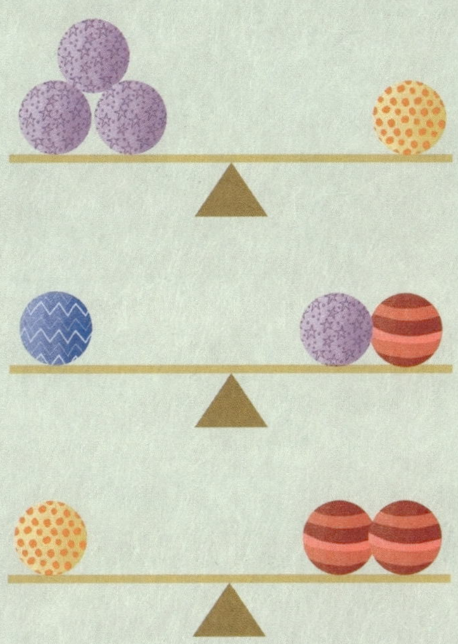

# The Second Law

This law explains how force is connected to the mass of an object and the acceleration of an object. Put simply, it is why it's harder to throw a heavy ball as far as a light ball. Use your mathematical brain to work out the mass of each of these balls.

# SPEED

Speed is a measure of how fast an object is moving. It's easy to work out if you know how far it has moved, and how much time that took. It uses this equation:

$$\text{speed} = \frac{\text{distance}}{\text{time}}$$

The most commonly used unit for speed in physics is m/second, but in everyday life you might see or hear Km/hour, miles per hour, m/min or others.

CALCULATE THE SPEED OF EACH OF THESE:

1. A person who runs 100 m in 20 seconds..................m/second
2. A car that travels 80 miles in two hours..................mph
3. A train that covers 180 Km in 90 minutes..................Km/minute
4. A tortoise that plods 8 feet in half an hour...............ft/hour

# Speed Trap

Speed cameras take two photographs of a vehicle and calculate its speed based on the time and distance covered. Follow the lines from the cars to the speed cameras to see which of these cars has broken the speed limit.

# Speedy Swimmers

Use the clues to work out which of the swimmers gets each position in the race.

The swimmer with the red hat beats the swimmer with the yellow hat by just one place.

The swimmer with the purple hat isn't last.

The swimmer with the green hat is three places behind the swimmer wearing red.

# FLOATING AND SINKING

Some objects float on water. Some objects sink. The difference depends on how dense an object is. Density is basically how tightly the material is packed inside an object. This is expressed scientifically as an object's mass divided by its volume. Think about an ocean liner—it's clearly very heavy, but it is not dense, so it stays afloat.

Look carefully and answer these questions.

1. What fraction of the boats have blue hulls?
2. What fraction of the boats have yellow and blue sails?
3. What fraction of the boats have sails with horizontal stripes?

# Abandon Ship!

A hole in the bottom of a boat will eventually make the boat sink, as the water replaces air, and the overall density of the boat becomes more than the density of the surrounding water.

Find which of these odd-shaped plugs will fill the gap to stop this boat from sinking.

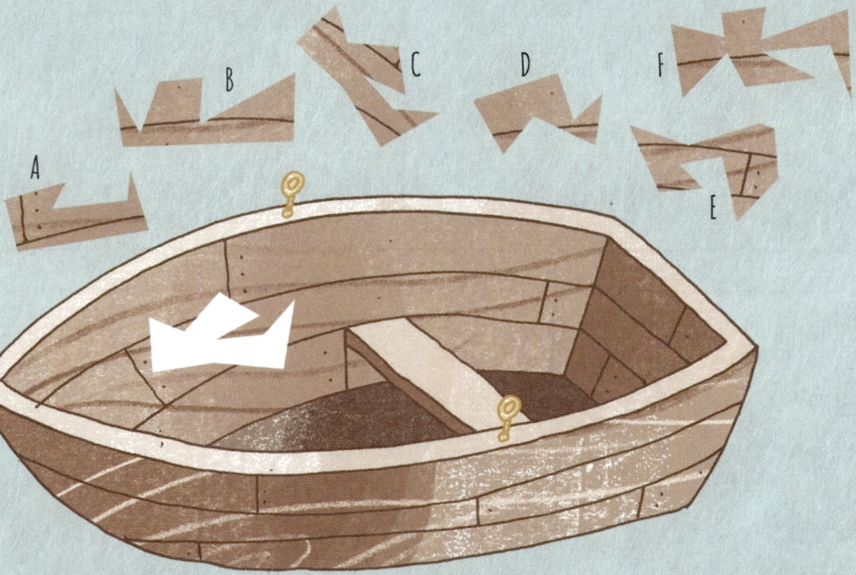


# Hydrophobic Oil

Oil and water don't mix because oil is a hydrophobic substance. When the two liquids are in the same container, the oil will float to the top because it is less dense. A thin film of oil on water (like you might see on a road or driveway) reflects the light in beautiful ways. See if you can find the three close-ups in the big picture.

# SIMPLE MACHINES

There are six types of simple machines: the wedge, the lever, the wheel, the screw, the pulley, and the inclined plane. Simple machines have very few moving parts. They use energy to perform the work needed.

Simple machines were likely to be the first inventions used by ancient people to make jobs easier. For instance, a chisel is a type of wedge, used to push two objects apart. It can be used for removing bark from trees, gouging out wood to make a canoe, and chipping stone into arrowheads.

Look at this cave drawing and circle all the tools you see that were weapons for hunting.

## Heavy Stuff

Possibly the simplest of machines is the inclined plane, or ramp—a flat surface with one end higher than the other. It allows us to slide heavy objects upward, rather than lifting them. It's thought that many ancient pyramids were built by moving large stone blocks on inclined planes.

A

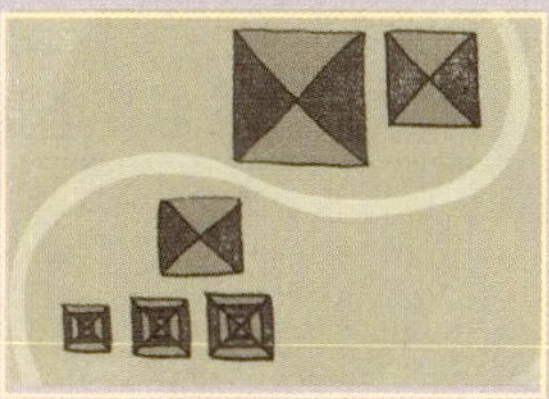

B

C

D

Study this picture of some Egyptian pyramids, and work out which of the smaller pictures is the correct overhead view of the same scene.

## Keeping it Together

A screw is also a simple machine because it is an inclined plane wrapped around a central pole. It can be used to hold things together or, if turned around and around, to lift things up.

How many screws can you count here?

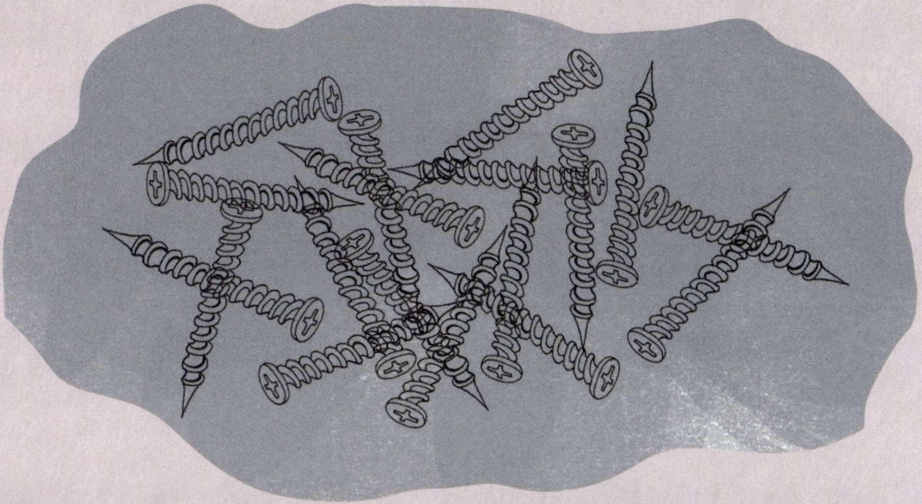

# THE WHEEL

The wheel is a type of simple machine (see pages 78-79) that, when combined with an axle, makes it easier to move things. Wheels were probably the last of the six simple machines to be invented, as the concept of a wheel fixed to an axle is a tricky one.

Early wheels were used not only on vehicles but also in windmills.

Look carefully and find a single wheel that's one of a kind.

## A Handy Helper

The first wheels weren't used for transport, but were potter's wheels, for making clay pots and bowls. Instead of making pottery by hand, the Sumerians developed the turning wheel so they could mass-produce their clayware. Which one of these pots is missing part of its design?

The Sumerians lived in Mesopotamia in Western Asia between 5,000 and 2,000 BCE.

## Turn it Around

Wheels with cogs, or notches, on the outside can be connected together. They can increase the force or the speed of moving objects. When two cogwheels (or gears) mesh together, it changes the direction of movement.

If Cogwheel A turns clockwise, which direction will the last cogwheel turn?

# TECHNOLOGY

Through history, inventors have used their science knowledge to create machines that made people's lives easier. Technology is amazing, and there's never been more of it than in this century.

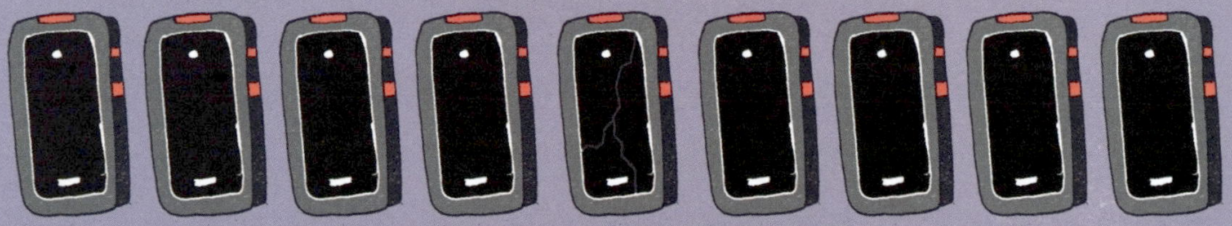

One of the major breakthroughs was the introduction of mass production. That allows us to produce goods in large numbers.

Look along the production lines here and find the defect in each row.

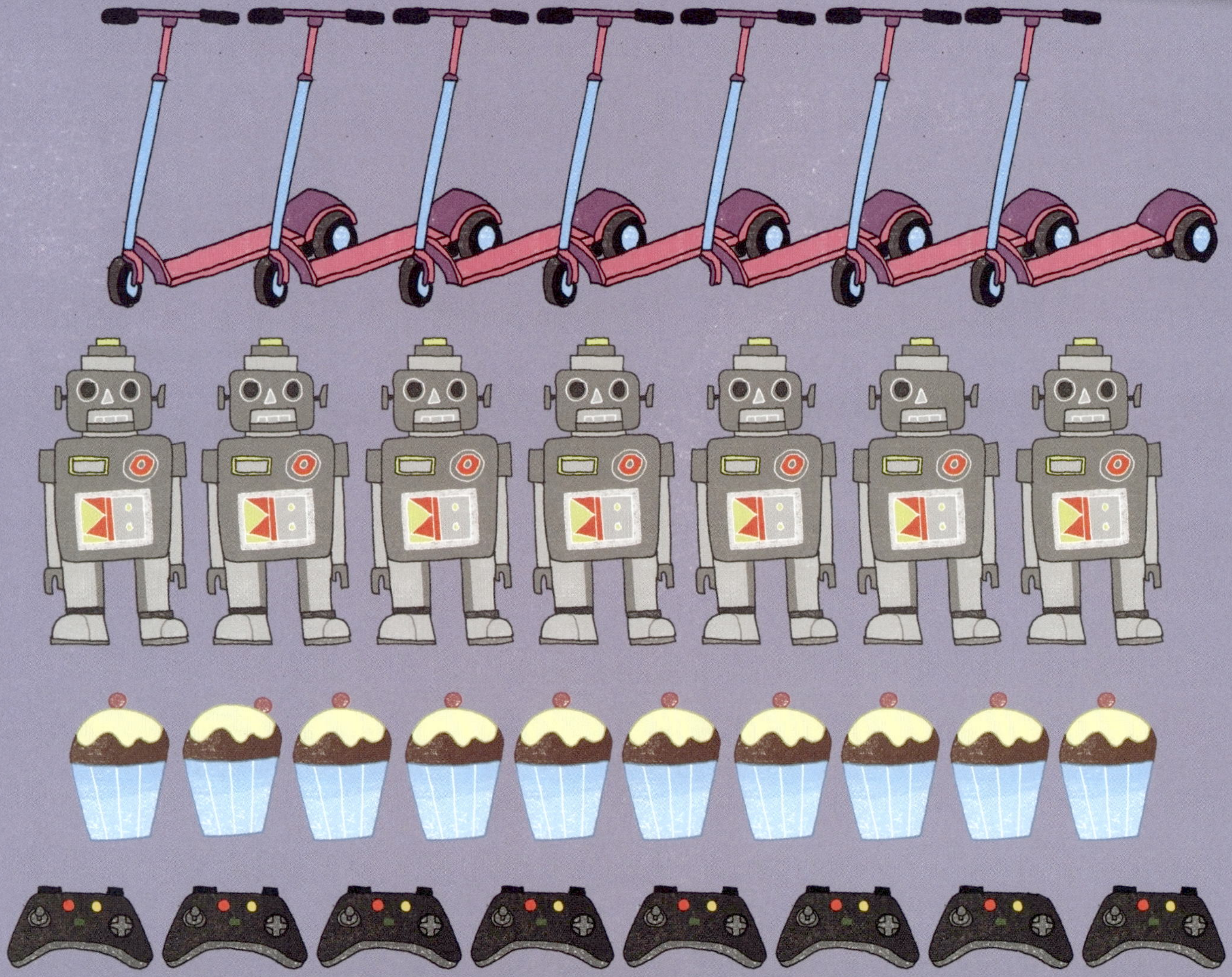

## Build Your Own

Movie robots resemble humans, and can often walk and talk. In industry, robots are more likely to be simpler machines that can do the same task over and over again.

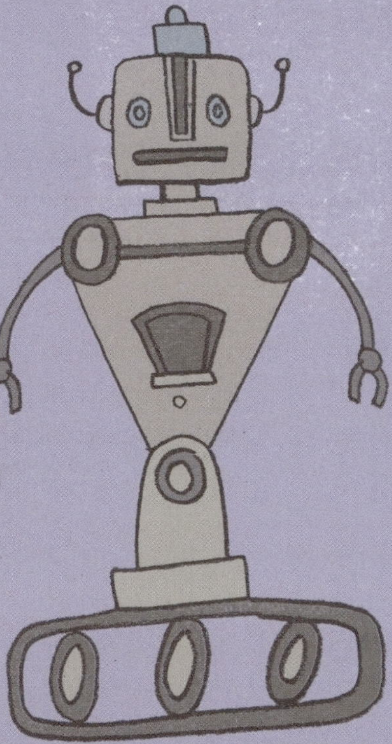

Which box of parts is needed to build another robot identical to this one?

A

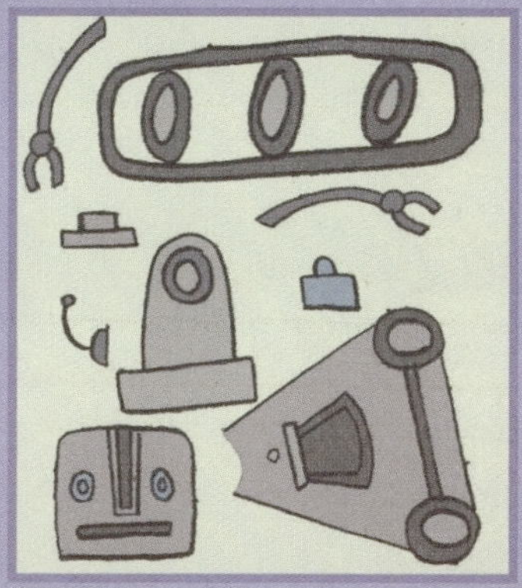

B

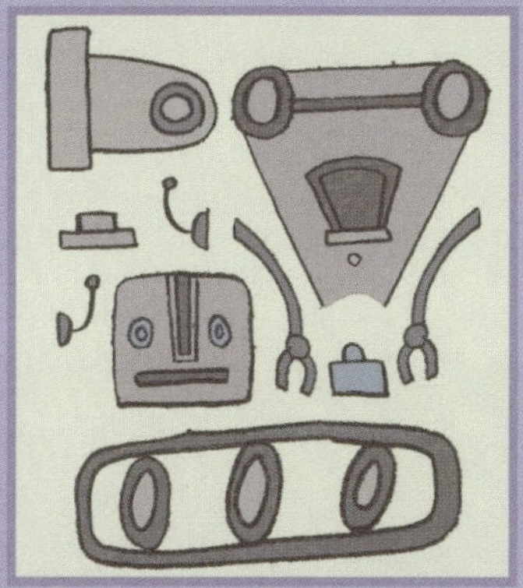

C

## Medical Marvels

Today's technology allows us to create amazing things. We can perform surgery on a tiny scale, and we can replace whole limbs or organs. Artificial limbs called prosthetics can be custom-made to match each person's abilities and requirements.

Which runner came first, A or B?

Runner A ran lap 1 in 40 seconds, lap 2 in 35 seconds, and lap 3 in 32 seconds.

Runner B ran lap 1 in 50 seconds, lap 2 in 29 seconds, and lap 3 in 27 seconds.

# OUT OF THIS WORLD

In the 1950s and 60s, the USA and the Soviet Union got caught up in a competition to see who had the best space technology. It became known as the space race. The Soviet Union was the first to send a person into space, in 1961. However, in 1969 the US succeeded in landing people on the Moon.

Saturn V was the rocket that launched the Apollo 11 mission to the Moon. Neil Armstrong was the first person to step onto the Moon's surface.

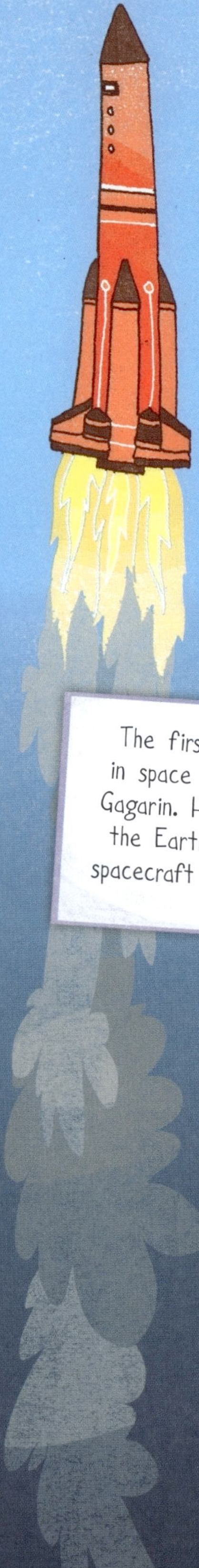

The first person in space was Yuri Gagarin. He orbited the Earth in the spacecraft Vostok I.

Start at the base of each rocket, and guide each of the spacecraft to its correct destination.

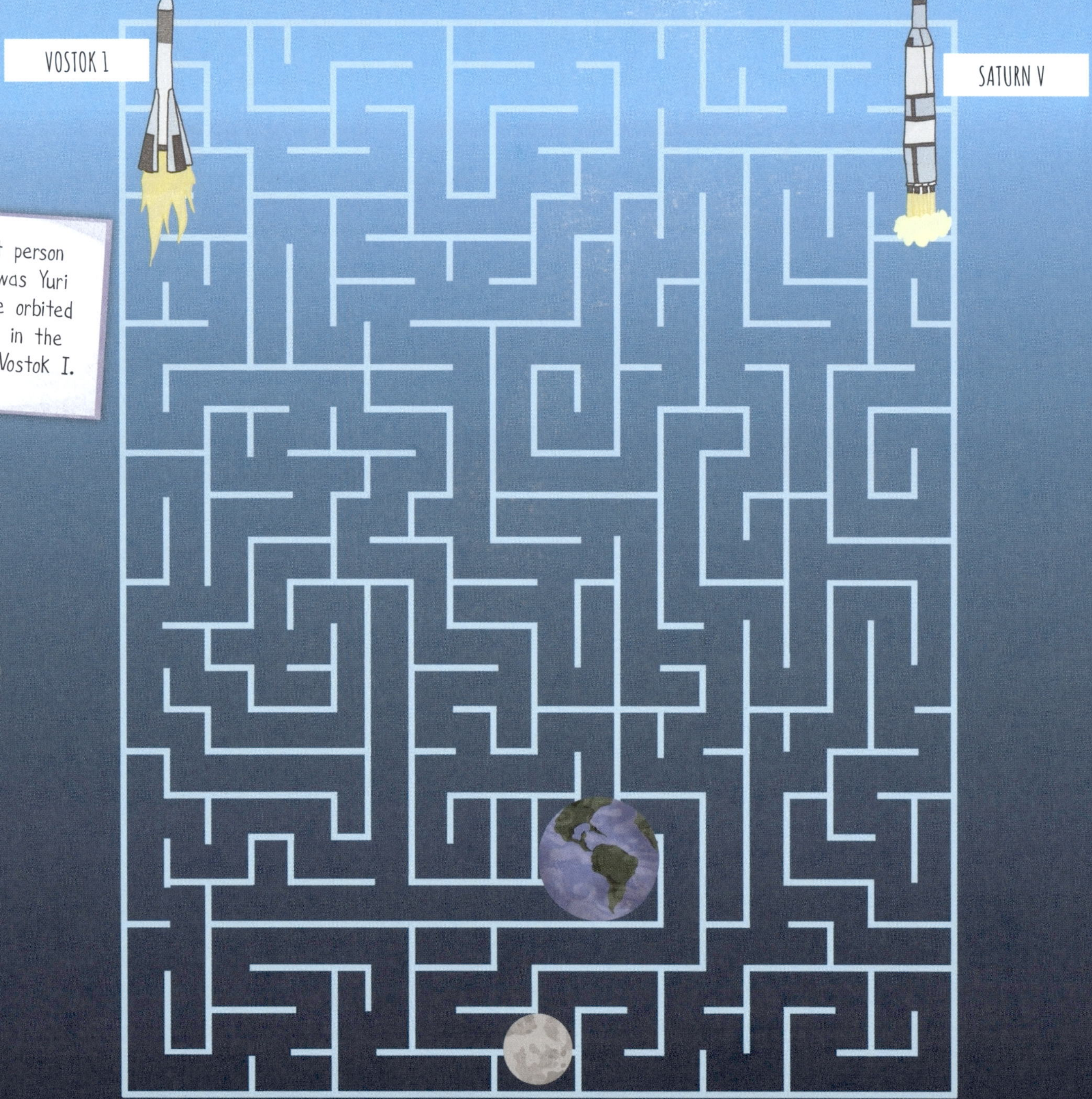

# Blast Off

Becoming an astronaut takes many years of training. Astronauts need to be good at science or engineering, learn survival skills, speak Russian and English, and be able to stay calm in an emergency.

Here, the astronaut must press the buttons in the correct order. Use the clues to make sure she gets it right.

Don't press B first.

Press A just before D.

Push F just before E.

Push C third.

Press A before only two other buttons.

# Space Signals

There are thousands of satellites orbiting the Earth. We have put them there to bounce signals from one side of the planet to the other, a bit like giant space mirrors.

Starting from the ground station, trace the signal from one satellite to the next. The first two signals have been done for you. If the signal always bounces off at 90 degrees, which is the last satellite it reaches?

# RENEWABLE ENERGY

The energy we use to power our homes, vehicles, workplaces, and schools can come from a variety of sources. Some energy is non-renewable, such as coal, oil, and natural gas. It will run out at some point. Renewable energy, such as wind, solar, or tidal power, can be replenished.

Some people have reduced the amount of non-renewable energy that they use by buying solar panels or electric cars.

1. What percentage of the homes here have solar panels?
2. What percentage of the houses still heat their home with fossil fuels? They're the ones with smoke coming out of the chimneys!
3. What percentage of the homes have a (green) electric car?

# LAND OF ICE AND...HEAT

Iceland produces more of its energy from renewable sources than any other country. Over 85 percent of houses in Iceland are heated with geothermal energy. Its water is heated underground and can be harnessed to make electricity.

Iceland has lots of active volcanoes and hot springs.

Cross out any letter that appears in ICELAND and use the remaining letters to spell the name of one of Iceland's most active hot springs.

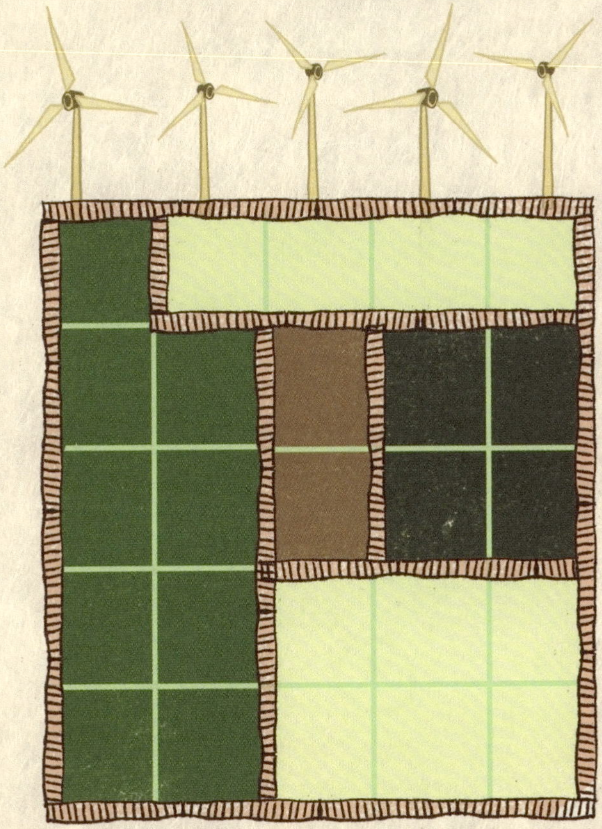

# WIND POWERED

Help the farmer plan where to place his five wind turbines. He must put one in each field, but there should be only one in each horizontal row or vertical column. He can't put two turbines next to each other up, down, across, or diagonally.

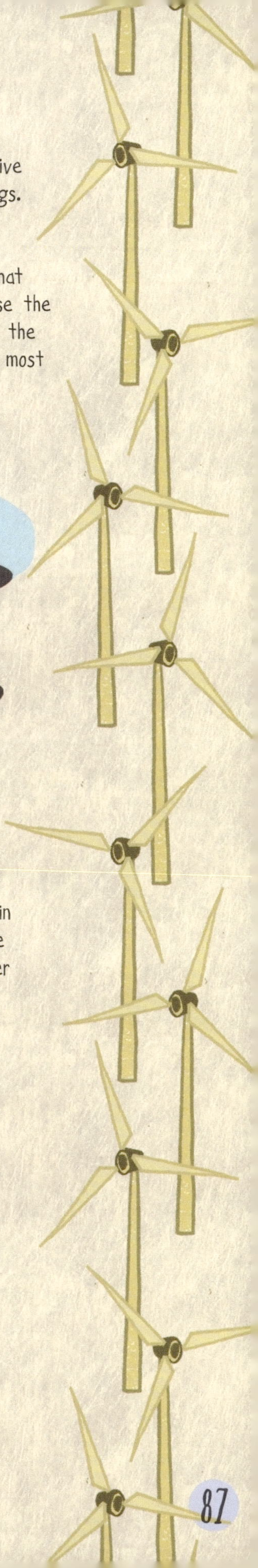

# CONSERVATION

It is important that we protect our planet and the things on it. This includes wildlife and natural resources such as water, forests, and soil. It is easy to overuse resources, or to pollute or destroy them.

Get conservation–clever by learning about what's good for the planet, and what's not. See what you can find in this mish–mash!

- SPOT SIX BICYCLES.
- FIND FIVE MILKSHAKE CUPS.
- SPOT SEVEN SHARKS.
- LOOK FOR FOUR RECYCLE SIGNS.

# Reduce, Reuse, Recycle

We can all try to lessen our impact on the world by reducing how much "stuff" we own and use, by using things again instead of throwing them away after a single use, and by recycling where possible.

Once we throw them away, some items hang around as waste for hundreds or thousands of years. Follow the lines to find out the frightening figures.

# Sustainable Fishing

As the world's population grows, we are taking and eating more fish from the oceans. We need to safeguard these oceans to make sure that there are enough fish in the future. Can you spot two fish in this shoal that are swimming in the opposite direction from the others?

# ANSWERS

## PAGE 6

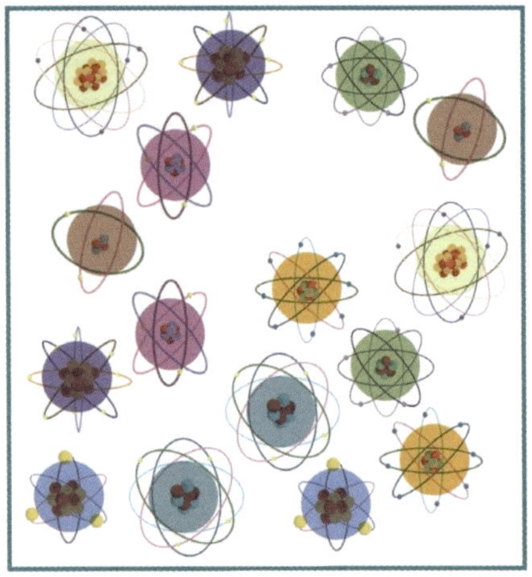

## PAGE 7

THERE ARE 3 MOLECULES OF WATER AND 4 MOLECULES OF CARBON DIOXIDE.

## PAGE 8

## PAGE 9

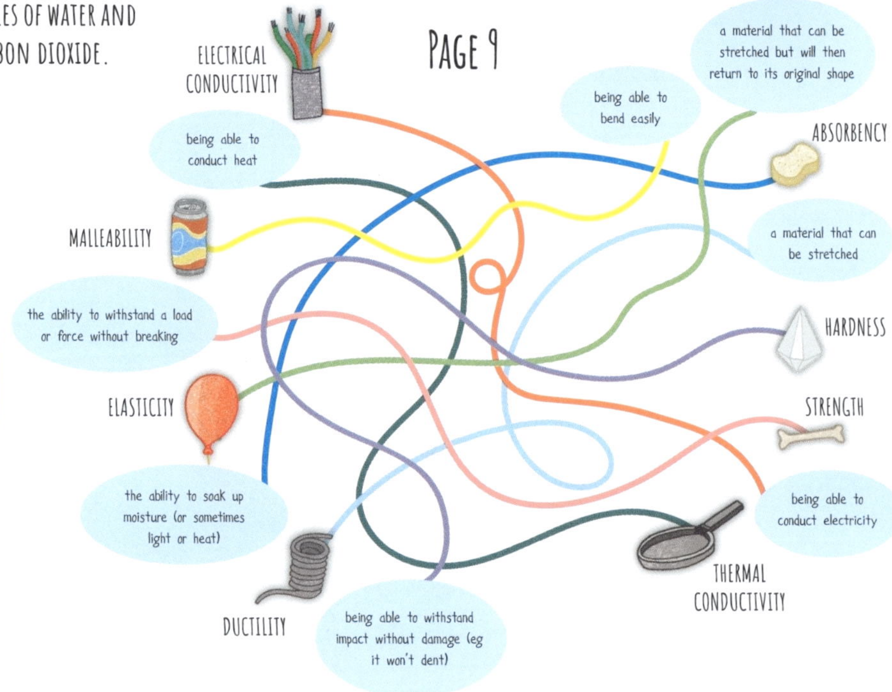


## PAGE 10

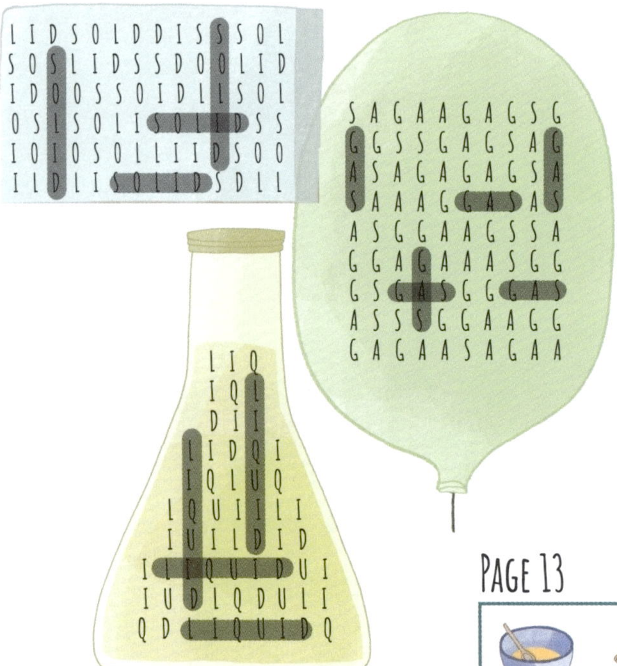


## PAGE 11

## PAGE 12

## PAGE 13

## PAGE 14

## PAGE 15

## PAGE 16

## PAGE 18

## PAGE 17

IN THE FIELD: TOOLKIT C, OCEAN GIANT: 276 TEETH

## PAGE 21

12 LIGHTBULBS

## PAGE 23

ELEPHANTS FROM LARGEST TO SMALLEST: F, B, C, E, D, A

MAKING WAVES:
5, 3, 6, 4, 7, 2, 8, 1

## PAGE 19

ABSOLUTE ZERO

## PAGE 20

IT TAKES 8 MINUTES FOR THE SUN'S LIGHT TO REACH EARTH.

## PAGE 22

PERCUSSION

## PAGE 24

| | BAKING | GYMNASTICS | GAMING |
|---|---|---|---|
| PAULO | | | ✓ |
| NANCY | | ✓ | |
| HENRY | ✓ | | |

| | YOUTH CLUB | SCHOOL | HOME |
|---|---|---|---|
| PAULO | ✓ | | |
| NANCY | | ✓ | |
| HENRY | | | ✓ |

## PAGE 25

CABLE B

## PAGE 26

THE DINOSAUR IS EXTINCT

## PAGE 27

KINGDOM
PHYLUM
CLASS
ORDER
FAMILY
GENUS
SPECIES

## PAGE 28

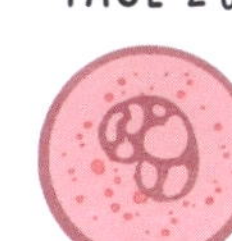

## PAGE 29

HYENA B HAS NO TWIN

## PAGE 31

| | | | | | | | | | | | |
|---|---|---|---|---|---|---|---|---|---|---|---|
| F | M | A | P | O | F | I | R | A | J | R | O |
| S | A | G | C | E | D | O | Q | O | Q | U | L |
| P | P | I | N | E | H | L | U | L | B | S | I |
| R | O | L | M | I | N | L | R | I | K | P | R |
| V | P | C | E | D | A | R | K | V | C | R | C |
| E | L | O | W | I | L | L | O | E | V | U | H |
| R | A | L | P | Q | A | S | H | O | S | C | D |
| B | R | L | H | H | E | L | T | T | E | E | T |
| O | F | Y | A | O | M | M | A | P | L | E | I |
| A | N | W | I | L | L | O | W | C | V | S | N |
| K | P | O | P | L | E | S | P | R | O | I | P |
| O | U | T | J | Y | T | B | I | R | C | H | I |

## PAGE 32

HEALTHY PLANTS: BAMBOO

## PAGE 33

## PAGE 34

## PAGE 35

B

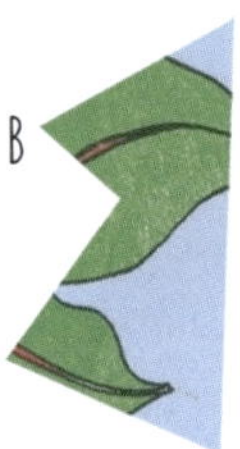

## PAGE 36

## PAGE 37

## PAGE 39

LEMURS B AND E ARE IDENTICAL

MIX AND MATCH

BAT – MAMMAL
FROG – AMPHIBIAN
EMU – BIRD
VIPER – REPTILE

TURTLE – REPTILE
RHINO – MAMMAL
SHARK – FISH
WHALE – MAMMAL

## PAGE 40

## PAGE 41

THE MOST POPULAR BREAD IS LOAF D

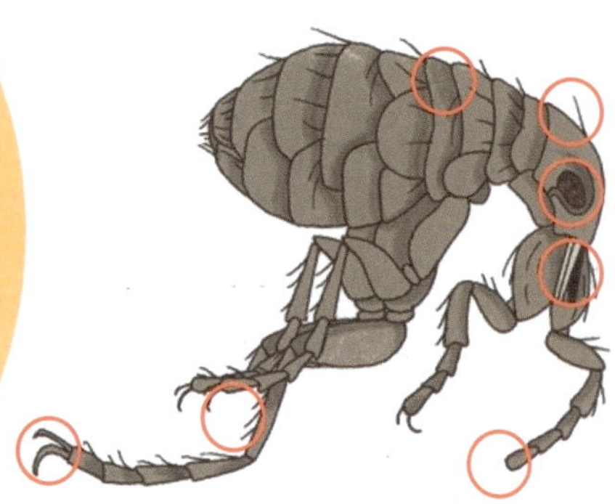

## PAGE 42

1. FRUGIVORE – TOUCAN
2. HERBIVORE – TAPIR
3. INSECTIVORE – ANTEATER
4. CARNIVORE – JAGUAR
5. OMNIVORE – MONKEY

## PAGE 43

## PAGE 43

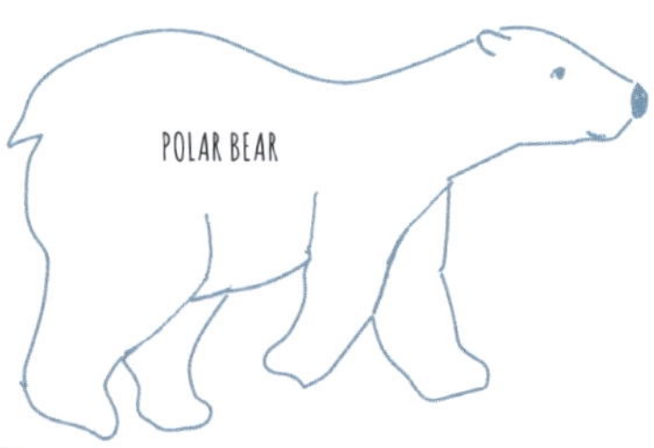


## PAGE 44

TUNDRA – REINDEER, ARCTIC FOX
SAVANNA – CHEETAH, OSTRICH
MOUNTAIN – SNOW LEOPARD, IBEX
FOREST – BEAR, BEAVER
RAIN FOREST – ORANGUTAN, PROBOSCIS MONKEY
GRASSLAND – BISON, PRAIRIE DOG

## PAGE 45

SILHOUETTE F

## PAGE 46

## PAGE 47

## PAGE 48

## PAGE 49

## PAGE 49

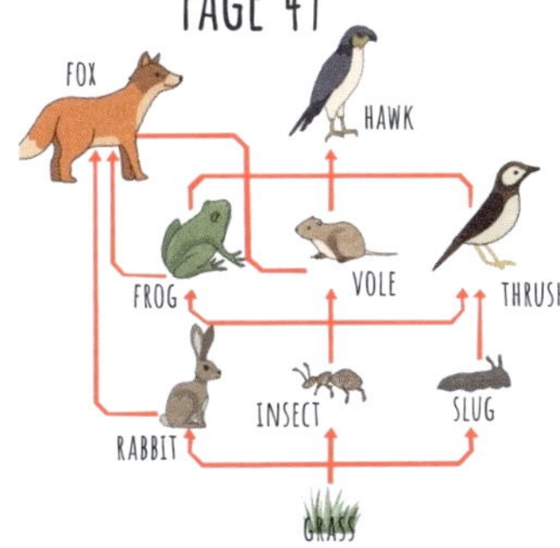


## PAGE 50

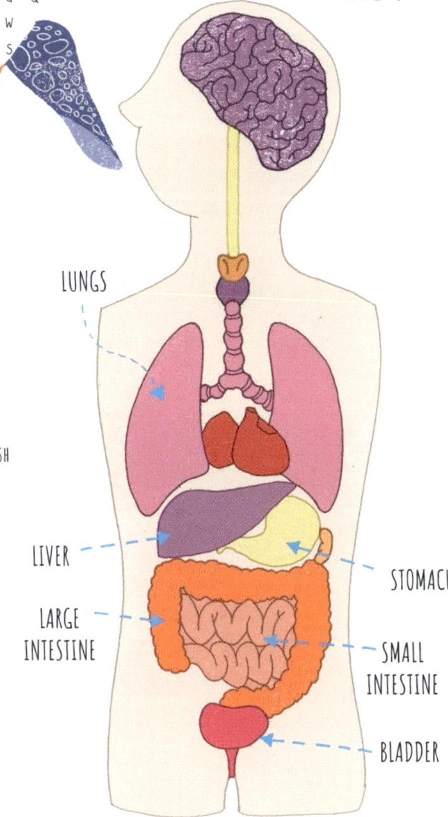


## PAGE 51

BONY BITS: 206 BONES

HIGH FIVE: FINGERS

## PAGE 52

SCAN D IS DIFFERENT.

## PAGE 53

THERE ARE 40 SQUARES IN TOTAL.

## PAGE 53

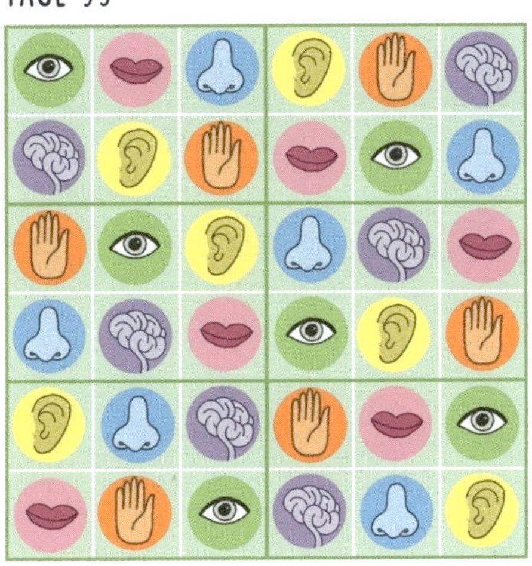

## PAGE 54

CARBOHYDRATES, FATS, VITAMINS, PROTEINS, WATER.

## PAGE 55

THE KIWI FRUIT AND PANCAKES HAVE BEEN EATEN.

## PAGE 56

1 = DECEMBER

2 = MARCH

3 = JUNE

4 = SEPTEMBER

## PAGE 57

BOTSWANA, ZAMBIA

BUILDING 1 NEEDS MAINTENANCE

## PAGE 58

INDIA

## PAGE 59

## PAGE 59

CLOUDY
SUNNY
RAINING
WINDY
SNOWING
STORMS

## PAGE 62

KIT TJ ROWAN MORGAN

SKIER = 55 CYCLIST = 46, THE SKIER GOES FASTER

## PAGE 63

THERE ARE 11 SPRINGS

## PAGE 64

## PAGE 65

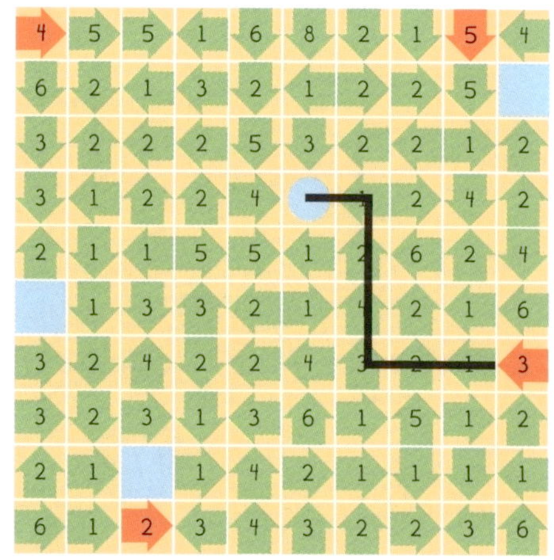

## PAGE 66

Newton's first name was Isaac. He was born in England in 1642. He is famous for his three laws of motion.

Einstein's first name was Albert. He was born in Germany in 1879. He is famous for his general theories of relativity. He is considered to be the most influential physicist of the 20th century.

## PAGE 67

## PAGE 67

JUPITER 115 KG (253 LB)
SATURN 48.5 KG (107 LB)
NEPTUNE 51 KG (112.5 LB)
MERCURY 17 (38 LB)
VENUS 41 KG (91 LB)
MARS 17 KG (38 LB)

## PAGE 68

## PAGE 69

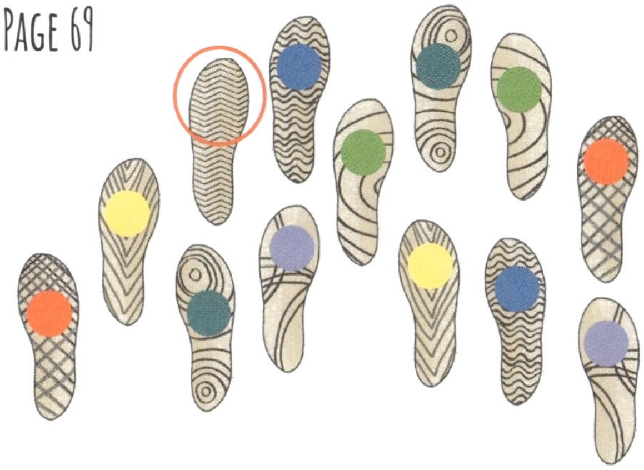

## PAGE 69

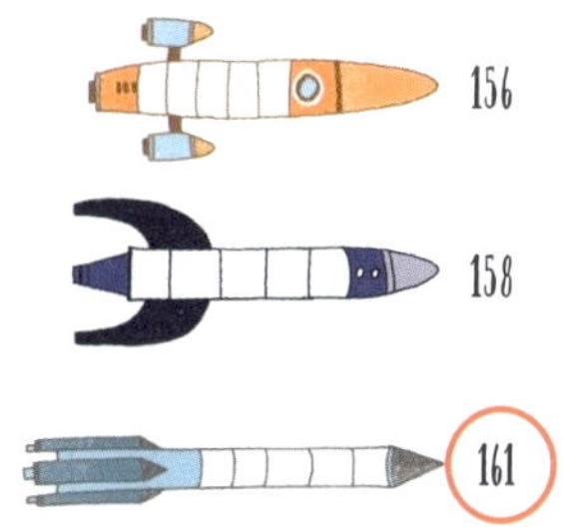


## PAGE 70

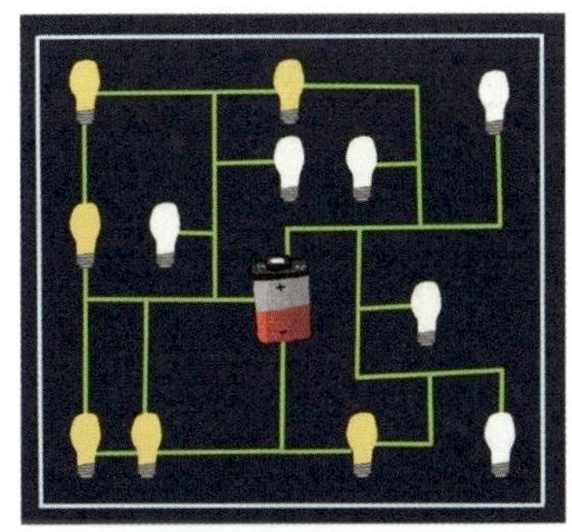

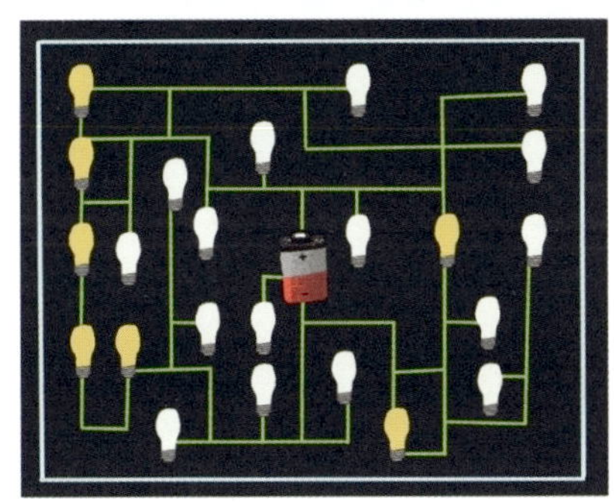

## PAGE 71

VENEZUELA

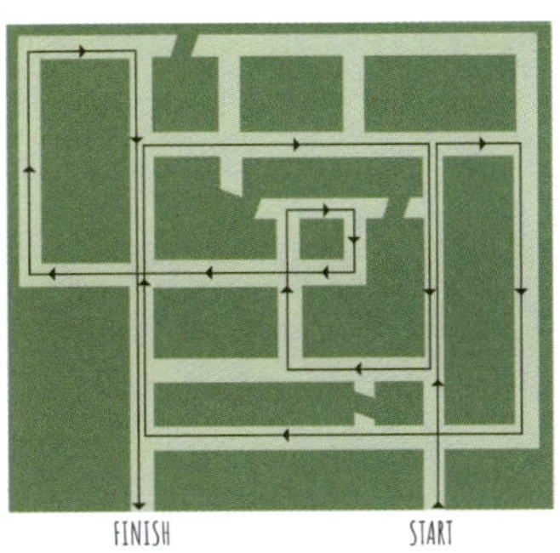


## PAGE 72

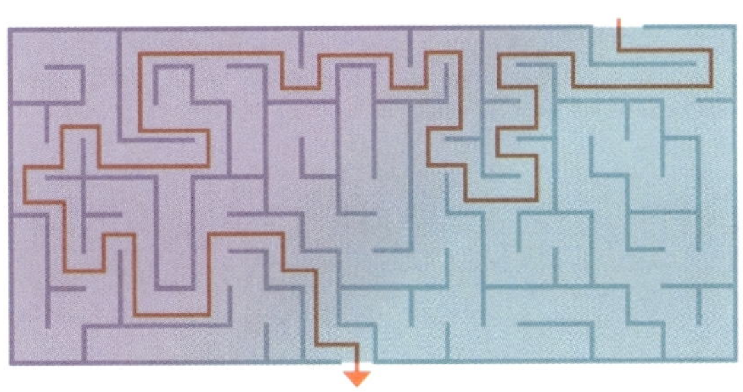

## PAGE 73

LAW OF INERTIA

## PAGE 74

1. 5 M/SECOND
2. 40 MPH
3. 2 KM/MINUTE
4. 16 FT/HOUR

## PAGE 75

SPEEDY SWIMMERS: RED, YELLOW, PURPLE, GREEN

## PAGE 76

1. $\frac{1}{4}$
2. $\frac{1}{10}$
3. $\frac{1}{5}$

## PAGE 77

PIECE C WILL FIT

## PAGE 77

## PAGE 78

## PAGE 79

PICTURE C IS CORRECT

KEEPING TOGETHER:
18 SCREWS

## PAGE 80

## PAGE 81

VASE F

TURN IT AROUND:
CLOCKWISE

## PAGE 82

## PAGE 83

BOX C

RUNNER B (106 SECONDS) BEAT
RUNNER A (107 SECONDS)

## PAGE 84

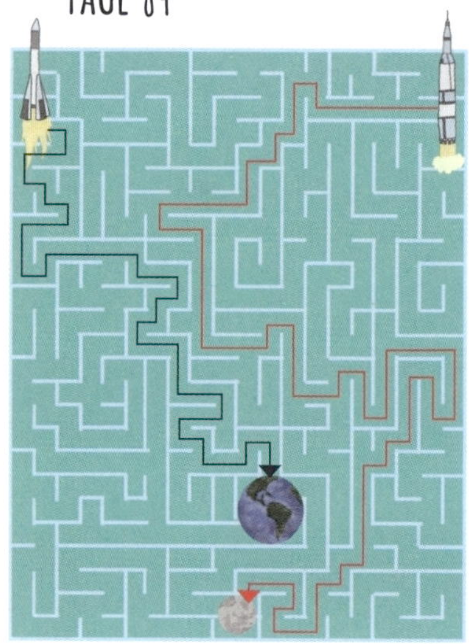

## PAGE 85

BLAST OFF: FECADB

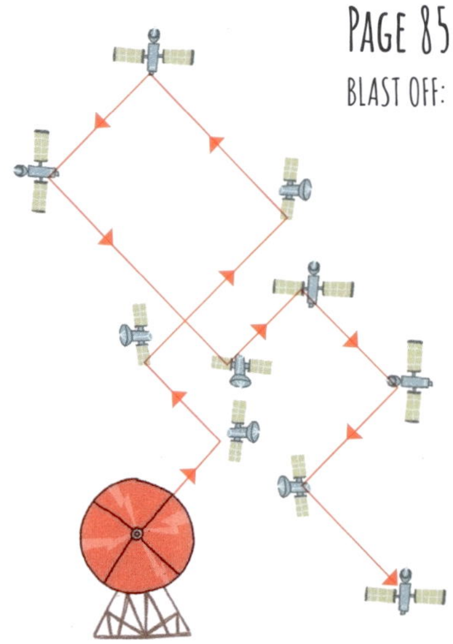

## PAGE 86

1. 50%
2. 15%
3. 30%

## PAGE 87

STROKKUR

## PAGE 87

## PAGE 88

## PAGE 89

STYROFOAM CUP - 500 YEARS OR MORE
GLASS JAR – 1 MILLION YEARS
DRINKS CAN – AT LEAST 200 YEARS
PLASTIC BOTTLE – 450 YEARS

## PAGE 89

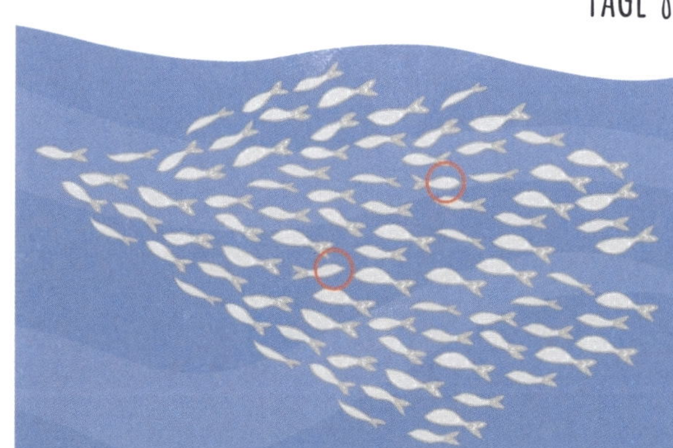